THE SHROPSHIRE HILLS
A WALKER'S GUIDE

ABOUT THE AUTHOR

David Hunter was for many years one of the great army of London commuters, working as a credit manager for a group of department stores and later as treasurer of a large advertising agency.

During this time he escaped whenever possible to walk in the Chiltern hills and the North Downs, and made frequent forays along the Ridgeway National Trail. He also wrote features for outdoor and other magazines, and developed his interest in photography, contributing to several photographic libraries.

David and his wife, Vera, moved to Worcester and began walking in the Malverns and around Bredon Hill and the hills south of Birmingham, as well as exploring the territory of the rivers Severn and Wye. He has a particular affection for Shropshire and the Welsh border country. David has had a number of books published, including five guides for Cicerone.

Other Cicerone guides by the same author

Walking in Worcestershire

The Offa's Dyke Path (Guide to the National Trail)

THE SHROPSHIRE HILLS
A WALKER'S GUIDE

by
David Hunter

2 POLICE SQUARE, MILNTHORPE, CUMBRIA LA7 7PY
www.cicerone.co.uk

© David Hunter 1991, 1997, 2004, 2008
Revised reprint 1997
Second edition, all colour, with OS mapping 2004
Revised reprint 2008
Text: David Hunter
Photography: David and Vera Hunter

ISBN-13: 978 1 85284 427 1
ISBN-10: 1 85284 427 2

A catalogue record for this book is available from the British Library.

Acknowledgement
I am indebted to local naturalists Sylvia Sheldon and Chris Bradley for some of the information in Walk 4.

Dedication
To my wife for reading and checking every word, walking every step of the way, identifying wild flowers and having patience above and beyond the call of duty.

Advice to Readers

Readers are advised that while every effort is taken by the author to ensure the accuracy of this guidebook, changes can occur which may affect the contents. It is advisable to check locally on transport, accommodation, shops, etc, but even rights of way can be altered. Paths can be affected by forestry work, landslip or changes of ownership.

The author would welcome information on any updates and changes. Please send to: info@cicerone.co.uk

Front cover: A walker's view of Carding Mill Valley, the Long Mynd

CONTENTS

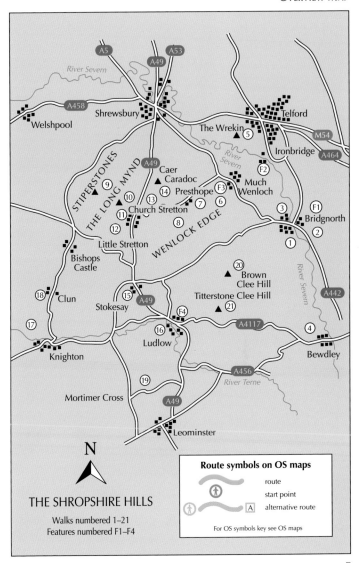

River Severn

A5   A53

A49

A458

Welshpool

Shrewsbury

Telford

The Wrekin

⑤

M54

Ironbridge   A464

River Severn

STIPERSTONES

THE LONG MYND

A49

Caer Caradoc

⑨

▲

⑩

⑬ ⑭

Presthope

F2

F3

Much Wenloch

Church Stretton

⑪

⑦   ⑥

③

F1

Bridgnorth

⑫

⑧

②

Little Stretton

WENLOCK EDGE

①

Bishops Castle

⑳

River Severn

▲ Brown Clee Hill

A442

⑱

Clun

⑮

A49

Titterstone Clee Hill

⑰

Stokesay

F4

▲ ㉑

A4117

④

⑯

Ludlow

Bewdley

Knighton

⑲

A456

River Terne

Mortimer Cross

A49

Leominster

N

THE SHROPSHIRE HILLS

Walks numbered 1–21

Features numbered F1–F4

Route symbols on OS maps

route

start point

A   alternative route

For OS symbols key see OS maps

7

Cliff Railway, Bridgnorth, from the east

PREFACE

In this tight little island of ours there is an astonishing variety of beautiful scenery, much of which remains relatively unknown. One such area is the Shropshire Hills and Severn Valley, which provides much good walking well within the capabilities of most people. It is a part of the country held in great affection by those who know it, but it seems clear that many people are unaware of the pleasures that could be awaiting them. This book, whilst not aiming to be an all embracing encyclopaedia on walking and exploring in this particularly attractive region between the Midlands and the Welsh Border, aims to distil a little of its essence by way of a series of walks across the area.

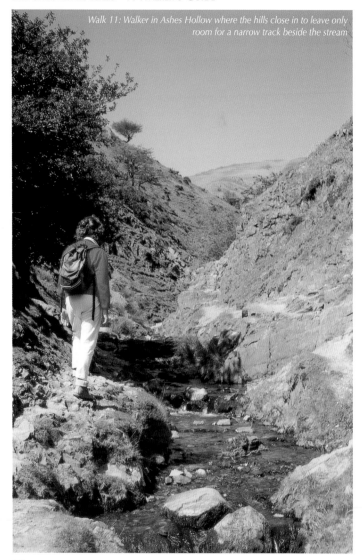

Walk 11: Walker in Ashes Hollow where the hills close in to leave only room for a narrow track beside the stream

INTRODUCTION

The territory to be explored is mostly in the Shropshire Hills Area of Outstanding Natural Beauty in South Shropshire, bisected by the A49 and centred on the little town of Church Stretton. No hard and fast rules are set, for we shall stray beyond these boundaries to visit Bridgnorth, a town neglected by many tourists, to enjoy the pleasures of the River Severn. Nor are we confined to the county of Shropshire, for we shall indulge in a little trespass into the neighbouring counties of Herefordshire and Worcestershire, including a walk through the ancient Wyre Forest and to sample Bewdley's river scenery. The pleasures of river walking will be contrasted with the high moors of the

Long Mynd, the sharp rocky spine of the Stiperstones, and the long windy ridge of Wenlock Edge. There is a magic ring to the very names of these places, and many have strong historical connections. At Knighton we shall be nudging into the Welsh Borders as Offa's Dyke is walked. The Clee Hills will provide us with the highest point in Shropshire, at 1772 feet, and here and there will be uncovered old superstitions, some not quite dead.

Much of the area is sparsely populated, and the names on the map may only indicate a remote hamlet or tiny village that happily has not grown with the times. Nor are the towns over large; their streets, pages in the book of architectural history,

Ludlow Castle, River Teme and Dinham Bridge

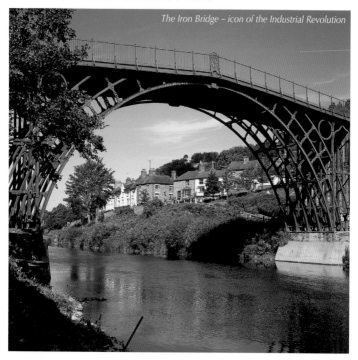

The Iron Bridge – icon of the Industrial Revolution

are a delight to explore: Ludlow is a prime example.

The landscape was shaped millions of years ago, it rises and falls in great rolling waves, and the walker may head off on a long ridge and enjoy the unfolding view as he rides the wave crest or plunges deep into the trough of the valley. The remains of ancient mining, as far back as Roman times, will be encountered and he can share a windy hill top with the ghosts of our long dead Celtic forebears. If you think this is

stretching the imagination a little too far, then suspend judgement until you stand on Caer Caradoc.

There is more than the hills and river valleys to be explored. There are the castles of Ludlow, Clun and Stokesay; the little village churches and the ancient priory at Much Wenlock. From the Wrekin's lonely summit the walker can look towards the birthplace of the famous iron foundries of Ironbridge, home of the Industrial Revolution. Ironbridge needs a day to itself at the very least, with its wealth of history; it is unquestionably one of the finest days out for all the family in the Midlands.

It is not only the past that can be enjoyed. There are other delights, not so easily located, less certain in the timing of their experience, but equally lasting in the mind of memorable days' walking. The swift blue flash of a kingfisher speeding across the brown waters of the Severn or the sight of a heron, that most patient of fishermen, standing as still as a garden ornament by the waters of a little brook. To this add the thrill of seeing the high soaring buzzards hunting along the scarp or catching a glimpse of a small group of deer, those elusive shadows of the forest.

All this is just to sketch in the scene, to whet the appetite, but attention must be given to the logistics of getting there, being properly equipped to enjoy the day and not being unduly burdened with the anxieties of finding the way.

GETTING THERE

Those with their own transport will not be faced with any problem, but those without a car do not have too great a disadvantage. A little careful homework on local travel facilities is of course essential.

- National Rail Helpline 0845 7484 950
- Buses 0870 608 2608

Severn Valley Railway in steam at Bridgnorth

- National Express Coach Services
  0870 580 8080

Tourist Information Centres and libraries usually hold local timetables, as, of course, do bus depots.

The Shropshire Hills Shuttle Service may be just what you need. It operates on three interchangeable routes from early April to the end of October. Routes include Carding Mill Valley and the Long Mynd, The Stiperstones, Clun and The Secret Hills. Contact 01588 673 888 for information and a leaflet. It is also useful to note that there are network railway stations at Shrewsbury, Church Stretton, Craven Arms, and Ludlow. Nor should the Severn Valley Railway be forgotten, operating between Bridgnorth and Kidderminster. There is more information about this later in the book.

MAPS

The relevant sheet number of the Ordnance Survey map, both 1:50,000 and 1:25,000 scale, is given for each walk. Regular walkers will find these a useful investment in making changes to routes and extending or curtailing a walk to suit the day's conditions. It is also helpful in planning other expeditions if crossing paths, not on the scheduled route, are checked for quality and destination. One of the many pleasures of walking is the time spent on some high point with a map spread over your knees picking out distant landmarks, putting a name to a misty hilltop or village spire.

Excellent as the OS Maps are they cannot guarantee easy walking. Paths that are writ large upon the map are sometimes ill-defined on the ground, have been subject to diversion, or

Walkers in a huddle, Offa's Dyke Path

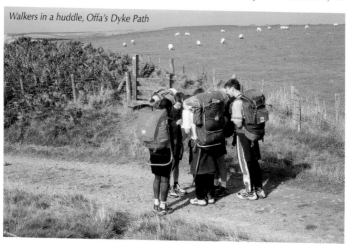

having fallen into disuse have been replaced by unofficial but locally accepted alternatives. No map maker, however good, can totally keep up with the changes. The best map for the walker is undoubtedly the 1:25,000 scale (2½ inches to the mile) Explorer map. It provides an immense amount of detail and is particularly useful in determining the passage of paths through fields, for example, by clearly showing which side of a boundary fence the walker can legally follow. The appropriate sheet number is quoted in the information panel at the start of each walk.

The obvious adjunct to navigating is a compass. At first sight this may not seem all that essential, but I have used one as much in the lower hills and in forest walking as I have in the high fells of the Lake District. A little time spent learning the principles of map reading and compass navigation will pay rich dividends, avoiding the frustrations, not to say embarrassment, of getting lost. The best of walkers stray from their intended path on occasion but intelligent use of the map will quickly correct the situation. Remember also that some of the walks described are in upland areas where low cloud and mist can envelop the walker and obscure landmarks. Here is just the situation where carrying a compass and having the confident ability to use it is very reassuring. The introduction of the Global Positioning System (GPS), now at an affordable price, is of course a valuable asset, but only if the user is already familiar with the principles of navigation.

WAYMARKING AND SIGNPOSTING

It is the practice to mark the points where footpaths or bridleways leave the road with metal or wooden signs. These may not always be in position but a programme of work over the past few years has improved matters. Advice from the Rights of Way Department was 'Unless challenged, walkers should assume that the rights of way are as shown on the current OS maps, irrespective of whether they lack signposts or waymarks'. Yellow

Footpath signing on the Long Mynd

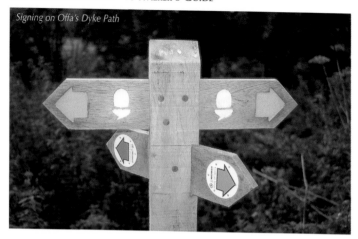

Signing on Offa's Dyke Path

arrows indicate footpaths, blue show bridleways. Additionally certain routes may carry special waymarks – National Trails (formerly known as Long Distance Paths) like the Offa's Dyke Path will have the acorn symbol of the Countryside Agency. Similarly regional routes such as the Shropshire Way which will also be encountered uses a buzzard as its symbol. Other long distance routes are Wild Edric's Way, marked by a sword, the Mortimer Way, and for those on horseback or mountain bike, the Jack Mytton Way. Such routes are usually waymarked throughout.

WHAT TO WEAR

The outdoor leisure clothing industry has produced a wide variety in price and style of apparel. A common sense approach will provide the equipment

suitable to the purpose and pocket. The aim is to be comfortable at all times – keeping cool, keeping warm, keeping dry, well shod with layers of clothing that are easily put on or stored away in a rucksack. A medium sized rucksack should suit most needs, although family walkers with young children may favour one of the larger, backpacker's variety. The proper packing and strap adjustment can be a great aid to comfort. As well as food, make sure you take plenty of liquid. Carry some basic first aid equipment – sting relief, insect repellent, sticking plaster, triangular and crepe bandages, etc. Don't forget sun block too. A small torch is useful when daylight hours are short and a whistle for emergency use (six short blasts followed by six long blasts is a recognised distress signal). A mobile phone may bring a speedier response but beware, the hills may harbour some dead spots.

What to wear is a matter of individual taste but wind and waterproof top garments are important and that should include waterproof trousers. Light or heavyweight shirts according to season, a good v-necked jumper, fleeces and body warmers are all very popular. Headgear, even if you normally go hatless, is important: wool or fleece bobble hats for winter and a light, brimmed hat as a protection on those occasions when the sun

suggests that we are in warmer climes than that to which we are generally accustomed.

Footwear is the single item that requires most care in selection. Whilst strong shoes or trainers will do for some of the walks, boots are generally needed. If you are buying for the first time don't be put off by the high prices of some specialist makers. Excellent as their products are you do not need to buy at the top of the range to find perfectly satisfactory boots that, with proper care, will give long

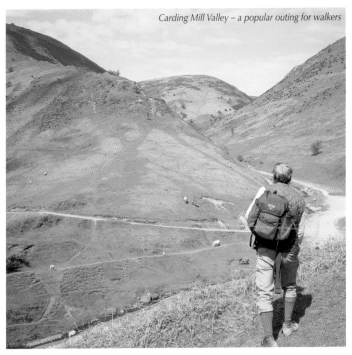

Carding Mill Valley – a popular outing for walkers

service. Look for padded ankle tops, sewn in tongues, quick release laces and good sole grips. Take your time when in the shop, checking for all the points mentioned and search for any unevenness or protruding nails which will become quickly apparent after a mile or two's walking. Despite the difficulty there may be in fully waterproofing some lightweight boots, I go for these where conditions are not going to be too muddy, reserving my medium weight leather boots for winter walking. Leather is not in itself waterproof, but regular attention with Nikwax and similar products should ensure dry feet. Wet feet in summer can be endured, on a frosty winter's day they are quite another matter.

CHILDREN

Children of all ages enjoy the adventure of a country walk and their stamina is surprising, but don't overstretch them. Toddlers and young babies are sometimes transported in papoose carriers. These are very useful in liberating young parents and allowing them to pursue the pleasures of country walking and are little more trouble than carrying a rucksack. There are however dangers, whilst the exercise may be keeping you at a comfortable temperature, the static child can become cold to the extent of hypothermia. Likewise overexposure to the sun has obvious dangers; sensible clothing and regular checks avoids the problem.

WHEN TO WALK

The routes described in this book can be followed throughout the year, subject to extremes of weather, such as the extensive flooding that sometimes occurs along the Severn, or possibly dangerous snowfalls in the hills – seemingly much rarer these days. Each season has its offering and there are not many days in the year when a walk is totally out of the question. Spring with its light breezes, the greening of the trees and the fresh wild flowers, is a delightful time of the year. Summer brings blue skies, high white clouds and the colours of the ripening harvest, and in August the heather covered summits of the Long Mynd become a vast purple carpet. Autumn, perhaps one of the best seasons for the walker, with its dramatic colouring of trees and bracken turning to a deep bronze, leads one to the enjoyment of winter walking. The shorter days produce their own particular pleasures: the crunch of boot over frost hardened ground, stormy skies adding interest to the landscape and woods freed from the veil of their foliage give up some of their secrets, whilst the study of tracks left in soft mud may give hope of the sight of deer round the next corner – in this connection to travel silently is to travel hopefully.

We learn as we go, becoming self taught in elements of bird recognition, wildlife and related nature study. Walkers with an enquiring mind will gradually acquire a small library of

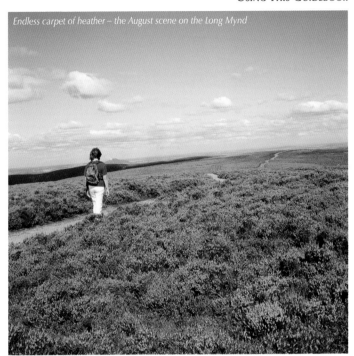

Endless carpet of heather – the August scene on the Long Mynd

books. Amongst those that I have found useful are the Collins Field Guides to trees, birds, insects and mammals and similar publications.

New legislation of the 'right to roam' variety continues to be of interest and may be destined to have a considerable effect on improving access to the countryside, particularly in upland areas. All the walks in this book are, to the best of the writer's knowledge and belief, on public rights of way or permissive or generally accepted access.

USING THIS GUIDEBOOK

Information about nearby places to visit is offered at the end of many of the walks. Opening times are given as a general guide and may be subject to change. Check in advance if you're making a special visit.

Further information about text in bold may be found in a side bar or information box.

Bridgnorth rises from the River Severn to St Mary's Church – architect Thomas Telford

WALK 1
Severn Down

Maps:	1:25,000 Explorer 218 Wyre Forest & Kidderminster Bridgnorth; 1:50,000 Landranger 138 Kidderminster & Wyre Forest area
Distance:	6 miles or 8 miles approx
Car parking:	Low Town off A442 near Fox Inn, on east bank of River Severn (grid ref 721929)
Toilets:	Opposite Fox Inn

Basic Route: Bridgnorth, west side Severn down stream, Daniel's Mill, Hampton Loade (or extension to Highley) return by Severn Valley Railway (check if it's running, see information box at end of walk)

From the car park turn left along the A442 and after short distance turn left again – soon to cross the bridge over the Severn. The clock tower on the right was erected in 1949 to commemorate the contribution to science and engineering by Richard Trevithick and John Rastrick whose first passenger locomotive engine was built only a short distance away in 1808. Immediately ahead, Bridgnorth's largest advertisement, covering an entire wall, hits you straight in the eye. It carries the proud message that S. E. & A. Ridley Ltd, established in 1616, are the oldest firm of seedsmen in Great Britain, supplying clover, grass, root and grain seeds.

As the walker advances over the bridge the prospect of High Town opens up. To the right is the sandstone tower of St Leonard's Church, around which houses are perched on the cliff that falls steeply towards the river. To the left is Telford's handsome church of St Mary Magdalene. Below, on the river bank, there is always a large congregation of white

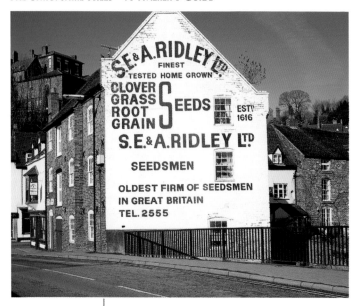

Ridley's ready made poster site

doves, mallards and some Canada geese enjoying the liberality of the duck feeding public.

Once over the bridge turn left to follow the river, gaining the bank through a small paved park. The Severn is now closely followed all the way to Hampton, with the exception of one small, voluntary diversion. As Castle Mount falls back the Severn Valley Railway's station is seen and, behind that, the top of Pan Pudding Hill, leaving little doubt as to the origins of its name.

Daniel's Mill

It is common for a local history to record that 'there has been a mill on this site since before Domesday' and Daniel's Mill is no exception. The mill has been in the present owner's family for 200 years, it was in full time working up to 1957 processing animal feeds. Prior to that it operated as a flour mill. Since the death of the miller in 1957 a great deal of careful restoration work has been done and today the mill is again grinding flour, following the centuries old tradition.

Bridgnorth is soon left behind. Shortly after passing under the concrete span of the bypass a wooded area is entered but the path keeps close to the river bank. In just over ¼ mile from the bypass a footbridge takes the walker over a little stream. At this point a turn to the right and over the road will enable a visit to be made to **Daniel's Mill**, the entrance to which is marked by an old millstone.

Note: map continued on page 26

The water to power the mill comes from the Potseething Spring, rising about ½ mile away near Coomsley. This spring was reputed to have a mineral content that was soothing to those suffering from sore eyes. The Severn Valley Railway is carried on a viaduct high above the millpond, a good opportunity for photographers if a train is passing. The mill wheel is the largest on a working corn mill in this country. Measuring over 38 feet in diameter and weighing a ton a foot, it clearly needed a fine degree of engineering design and construction to ensure smooth running. Part of our industrial

23

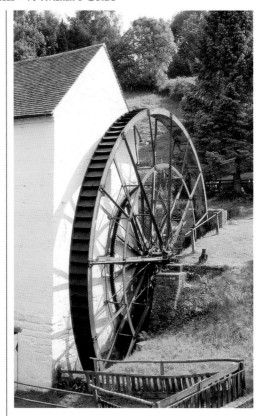

The giant waterwheel at Daniel's Mill, Eardington

heritage, it is made from cast iron and dates from 1854. It was built at the famous Abraham Darby's Coalbrookdale forge. The mill is open to the public (see information box at end of walk) and by way of a souvenir you can buy a bag of stoneground wholemeal flour and have a stab at making your own bread.

After visiting the mill retrace your steps and continue downstream. At first the path is very close to the river edge and, as it can be slippery after wet weather, some caution is needed. The path opens up again to more comfortable walking and the wooded sandstone cliffs of Cliff Coppice can be seen ahead.

The river is busy with wildfowl and the trees edging the river provide a good feeding ground for birds; blue tits and great tits are particularly active. There are kingfishers about and I have rarely failed to see one, however briefly. Herons are also likely to be seen.

Nearly 2 miles downstream from Bridgnorth you'll pass Quatford, on the opposite bank. Its more visible features include Quatford Castle, a battlemented residence built in 1830, and the high bluff that nudges forward to the river. Long ago this commanding position was the site of a motte and bailey. Beyond it lies the sandstone parish church.

Progressing downstream it is not long before a tall chimney announces the little settlement of Lower Forge. On reaching the hamlet a tunnel can be seen cut from the sandstone cliffs, a relic of the days when the forge was busily engaged in the manufacture of nails. The tunnel accommodated a canal cut from Astbury to carry iron ore by narrow boat to the works. The boats were 'legged' through the tunnel with the finished product being returned the same way or by horse and cart along the lanes. In recent years a canoeist (bold fellow) attempted a passage through the tunnel but the waterway was partly blocked and he was obliged to haul his canoe over a rock fall.

Charcoal burning was a local occupation and trees in the area were coppiced for the purpose. A small diversion up the track from the river will provide a view of this tiny iron-making settlement. The white building was both the pay office and the manager's house, with near by a row of eight cottages for the workers. The owner of one of the cottages told me that according to his lease he is still obliged to pay two shillings and sixpence (25p) per annum for the right of passage for a horse and cart over the farm roads. The largest house, Severn House, is partly built into the sandstone.

Continuing along the bank a bridge over the Mor Brook is crossed and the high banks of the Chelmarsh

Reservoir are seen to the right. High tree covered cliffs rise here and there along the river, and little streams add their widow's mite to the waters of the Severn. Near Hampton Loade a bright blue bridge arches across the river, it is the property of the Severn Trent Water Company and not open to the public. This is a pity as there are a very limited number of bridges and to be able to cross here to join the footpath on the opposite bank would be useful to walkers.

A little further on as Hampton is reached a ferry operates but it cannot be relied upon at all times, since flood conditions may restrict its operation – it sank during the heavy floods of November 2000! A bell to summon the ferry is found on a telegraph pole, not that we need to cross the river on this excursion, but it offers possibilities in planning future riverside walks. Just beyond the ferry you'll reach a lane, and here you have two options.

Route A: Continue downstream for a further 2½ miles to take the train back from Highley (when operating: see information box at end of walk). It is pleasant walking with trees edging the banks here and there. When the Colliery Bridge is reached it is worthwhile leaving the bank for a moment to take in the view from above of the river within its wooded setting. Coal was being mined at Highley Colliery until the 1960s. The spoil heaps across the river have been landscaped and now form part of the Severn Valley Country Park project which extends to both sides of the river. The west side can be reached from Highley

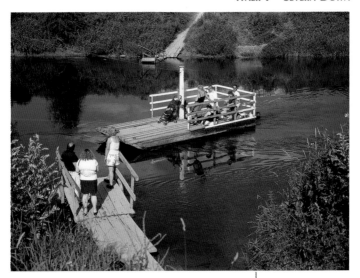

The Severn Ferry at Hampton Loade

Station. Highley Village stands on the top of the hill and about ½ mile from the station. It pays tribute to its heritage with a modern sculpture of a miner descending in a pit cage. The car park for the country park is signed from the village. On the hillside is a wheel of the winding gear that took so many men to work in the pits.

Main walk contd: Those who feel that they have now walked far enough should make their way up the lane to Hampton Loade Station for the journey back to Bridgnorth by **steam railway**.

A railway between Shrewsbury and Worcester was first mooted in 1846 and seven years later the Severn Valley Railway Company was formed. Railway history is all too often a complicated matter, with familiar stories of shortages of money, amalgamations, engineering difficulties, and particularly in the 1960s, closures. Sufficient therefore to say that construction began in 1858 and 20 years on a link to Kidderminster had been established.

*Mining memorial
Severn Valley Country
Park, Highley*

From Kidderminster the traveller is off on a chug-ging, gently rumbling adventure, high above the world on embankments, diving deep into cuttings or vanishing into the blackness of Bewdley Tunnel. The scenic route follows the edge of the Wyre Forest, and travellers may be surprised at the sight of bison on the skyline until they discover that they are passing the West Midlands Safari Park. Progress is made at a comfortable pace, giving time to enjoy the scenery, even identify some of the wild flow-ers in the woods and along the embankments. For much of the way it keeps close company with the river with splendid views of the fast flowing Severn.

Stops are made at little country stations, crowded with more passengers than they probably ever saw in their strictly commercial days. At Bridgnorth, northern terminus of the line, there is freedom to walk round the engine sheds, where the locomotives are maintained and former rusting kings of the iron road are restored to health.

Steam Railway

As uneconomic lines were closed after the Beeching Report of 1963, preservation societies sprang up with the avowed intention of protecting and preserving at least a part of our great railway heritage. (The number is close to the 100 mark). The Severn Valley Railway Preservation Society was formed in 1965, operating on 16 miles of track between Kidderminster and Bridgnorth. Its enterprise encompasses seven stations, carriage and wagon works at Bewdley, with heavy engineering restoration and maintenance sheds at Bridgnorth. Christmas specials and steam gala days attract large crowds of enthusiasts from many parts of the country. Kidderminster station was constructed from a design for Ross-on-Wye Station of 1890, with a Victorian post box nicely setting the date. Enamelled advertising plates clamour for attention proclaiming the merits of some still familiar, and some forgotten, brands.

On leaving Bridgnorth Station a return to the car park can be made either crossing by steps or footbridge to Castle Mount, turning right to walk round the Mount, descending to Low Town by the Cartway or the Cliff Railway and over the bridge to return to the car park.

Severn Valley Railway engine sidings

*Just the way it used to be – Highley
Station on the Severn Valley Railway*

Tourist information: The Library, Listley Street, Bridgnorth Tel: 01746 763257

Severn Valley Railway: Timetable enquiries 01299 403816. Daily services May to Sep with other services earlier and later in the year

Childhood and Costume Museum: Postern Gate. Bridgnorth. Variable opening times

Bridgnorth Museum: Northgate. Open 11–4 Easter to Oct, Sat, Sun and bank holiday Mon. Extended opening during school holidays

Town Hall: Well worth a visit – limited opening – check on arrival but usually mornings from 11am

St Mary Magdalene Church: Open daily

Daniel's Mill: South of Bridgnorth off B4555. Open 11–4 Wed, Sat and Sun, Easter to end Sep. Bank holidays 11–6. Parties should call 01746 762753

Dudmaston Hall, Quatt: Off A442, 4 miles south of Bridgnorth. 17th-century house of Francis Darby of Coalbrookdale with extensive grounds and lake. National Trust property. Open from 2pm Tue, Wed and Sun, bank holiday Mon end Mar to end Sep

WALK 2
High Rock

Maps:	1:25,000 Explorer 218 Wyre Forest & Kidderminster Bridgnorth; 1:50,000 Landranger 138 Kidderminster & Wyre Forest area
Distance:	11 miles approx.
Car parking:	Low Town, off A442 near Fox Inn (grid ref 721929)
Toilets:	Opposite Fox Inn

Basic route: Bridgnorth, east bank of Severn downstream, Quatford, Stanmore, Hoccum, Roughton, Burcote Rocks, Rindleford, The Knolls, Batch Lane, High Rock, Hermitage Caves, Low Town

From the car park, turn left and, in a short distance, left again, signposted to Bridgnorth town centre. On reaching the bridge, turn left to follow the River Severn downstream on the eastern bank. From the riverside walk there are good views of Castle Hill beneath which are **Castle Hill Caves** once used as dwellings.

The southern end of the island in the river provides a haven for wildfowl. The feathered residents include Canada and greylag geese and the inevitable mallards. The Severn flows swiftly beneath tall chestnut trees whose branches dip down to the water, making a green protective canopy for the wildfowl and their young in season.

Castle Hill Caves
As well as being used as dwellings – there is one opening that was intended to serve quite a different purpose. During the Civil War there was an attempt by the Parliamentarians to tunnel through the easily worked sandstone into the town – a venture which probably says more for the enterprise and enthusiasm of the besiegers than for their consideration of practical strategies.

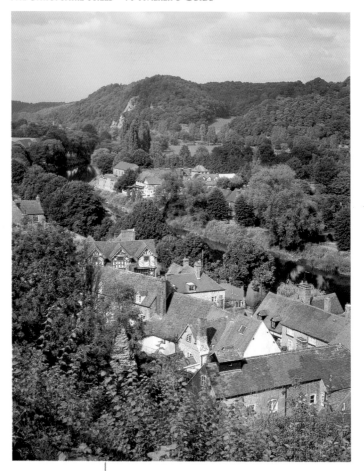

High Rock – a distant view from Bridgnorth

Follow the river, passing under the concrete span of the bypass, until it bends very close to the road at Quatford, just over 2 miles downstream from your starting point. Ahead can be seen the high bluff of Camp Hill and Quatford church. As houses are reached a stile is crossed to take a path sharp left, to reach the road after a few

yards, oppo-
site the old post
office. Cross the road and
walk up Chapel Lane as it climbs
away from the river, soon to leave the village behind.
(Note there is a path through Quatford Woods that might
be used to reduce the road walking a little.)

It is a quiet lane edged by woods with sandstone outcropping here and there. The sandstone has been inscribed in a literate, not to say artistic manner with initials, dates, words, even faces and symbols, but their meaning is not clear, leaving a small enigma for walkers to puzzle out as they make their way uphill. At the top of the hill the views open out to a gently rolling countryside of fields and low wooded hills.

When the T-junction with the A458 is reached cross the road to join a metalled lane opposite, which soon becomes a wide track. There is open country to the right and for a while the Stanmore Industrial Estate is bordered on the left. This is a sharp demarcation between country and industry, so much so that at one point my attention was divided by the deep red glow of hot metal from a

On High Rock – a view up the River Severn

forge on one side and the startled flight of a covey of partridges on the other.

Ignore the turning to the right as the factory sites begin to fall back and maintain your forward direction on a much narrower path with a hedge on the left and a wire fence on the right. The path widens again and, when a lane is reached, go forward towards Hoccum. From here we are following little used lanes giving the flavour of the country roads of the past.

When you reach Hoccum House follow the lane sharp right downhill, eventually to pass a house that still retains an old hand water pump in its front garden. When the road divides, ignore a turn to the right and continue forward, the garden of the house to the right is full of snowdrops in the early spring.

After passing Willowbrook Cottage on the left, a road is reached, turn left to make a junction with the A454. Turn right and cross the road. In a few yards join a path on the left at the foot of the steep roadside bank. Head diagonally left across a field to a stile, which is found between two willow trees.

Once over the stile and a tiny brook turn right following the path with a field boundary on your right. Cross a further waymarked stile, then turn left along the field boundary with a hedge on your left. Davenport House is seen on its hilltop site to the north east.

At the end of a large field pass through a metal gate with the path now swinging slightly to the left. At the top of a slight rise go forward towards a gate situated between a cottage and a barn. Once through the gate cross a short grassy paddock and over a further stile. Here turn right to take the path running behind the cottage. Pause at the stile for a moment to take a look at the brickwork of the barn with its pleasing patterning, worth a photograph if the light is right.

From here on we enter on the best of the walk, passing through similar but in their own ways, quite different environments, with contrasts of scale. One a small, almost secret, river valley, the other the more expansive scenery associated with the Severn.

Take the path that runs behind the cottage with wooded slopes to your left. Soon you are following a delightful terraced path high above the little River Worfe. As the path descends, cross waymarked stile and go forward with sandstone cliffs to your left. The path swings round the cliff and the way then crosses the stile by a large gate on the left to pass through the garden area of a white house, before crossing a cattle grid. Go forward on a metalled track to cross the river by a small hump backed bridge.

Pause here to take in the scene. You are in a narrow river valley, with the wooded heights of Burcote Rocks and Soudley Rocks walling in the gorge to create one of nature's hidden gardens. The tree lined banks of the river and the woods provide a sheltered habitat for birds. I once watched a heron glide gracefully up the stream to land just a few feet from where I stood.

From the bridge bear left along the track, with the river winding through the valley to your left, to reach Rindleford Mill in just over ½ mile. Do not go beyond the mill, but turn left as it is reached to cross the Worfe by way of a little wooden bridge. Follow the path upstream with the rock outcrops to your right. About 200 yards from the bridge take a track on the right which makes its way through the woods with high banks on either side.

The rising woodland track is followed for ½ mile to join Batch Lane which is followed for ¼ mile to reach a metalled lane. Here turn left and, in a few yards, take a signed footpath on the right; this is a wide track as far as Woodside Cottage where it narrows to run between hedges, busy with blue and great tits. On reaching the wood, about ¼ mile from the lane, turn left to follow a narrow but clear path along the inside edge of the wood. After a short distance a junction of paths is reached, take the right fork, which runs downhill but, after only a short distance, turn left up a stepped path to follow a narrow terraced path through the centre of the wooded hillside. The slopes to the right fall sharply away with the River Severn glimpsed through the trees, the veil which hides the view will shortly be thrown back as the walker arrives at a high bluff thrust forward to give an exciting prospect of the river.

It is a superb position with every incentive to stop for refreshment and enjoy the magnificent views at a giddy height above the road with the Severn immediately below. Upstream the river flows under the high wooded cliffs on the east, whilst on the west bank diminutive players people the golf course. Below are the towers of Fort Pendlestone, a fake military-looking building of the

Hermitage Caves – the easily worked sandstone that is characteristic of the area

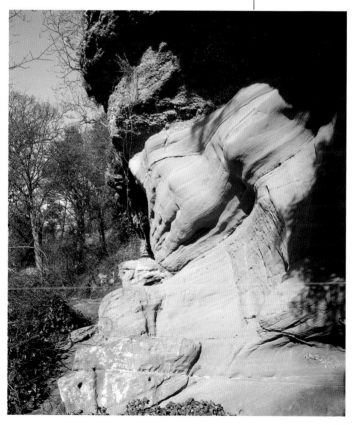

mid 19th century, built by William Whitmore of Apley Park whose house we shall see, at a distance, on the next walk. Downstream Severn Park is laid out, with little blue and white figures racing towards the matchstick-like posts of the rugby pitch. The eye is carried quickly to Bridgnorth on its commanding height.

At the day's end it is a rewarding place to pause and watch the fiery light of the setting sun spreading a great wash of orange behind the blackly silhouetted Clee Hills beyond Bridgnorth.

When the last of the rocky observation points is reached, the view somewhat occluded by its crown of Scots pine, and the rock much decorated with the initials of Bridgnorth's younger generation, a fish hook turn is made through the woods. From this last high point the path now swings to the left behind the rocky bluff. The terraced path should now be followed, still through the woods. As the path falls a little it bears to the right and then rises again, to join a crossing path coming in from the left, turn right with this. After 100 yards or so the path divides, take the left fork, (upper path) and continue forward to meet the road, having passed a reservoir on your left.

The road (B4363) is reached by a public footpath sign. Cross the busy road to join a path opposite that climbs steeply. Ahead are a series of large **caves** ◀. Local legend has it that a witch lived in one of these caves and took flight in traditional style each evening as darkness fell.

An inspection of the caves will show evidence of the working of the stone to create a small chapel-like chamber. Alfred's encouragement of learning is well known and it is interesting that this passed down to his grandson who decided to retire to these quiet caves to devote his time to a study of literature.

Having viewed the former retreat of the learned hermit, retrace your steps a few yards to take the path that runs along the inside edge of the wood above the caves.

About 100 yards after passing the green banks of a reservoir take the distinct path on the right, soon to meet

A rather more famous resident of the **caves** – and with some evidence to substantiate his existence – was a hermit, Ethelred, (or Ethelward); a grandson of Alfred the Great and brother of Athelstan, King of Wessex and Mercia, in AD 925.

a crossing path. Here turn right downhill to meet the edge of a wood; cross the stile and carry on through the field to the edge of a housing estate. On the skyline will be seen the long line of the Clee Hills and, nearer at hand, the now familiar prospect of Bridgnorth's High Town.

Make your way through the housing estate; at the end of the first road, Hazel View, bear right; at the end of Oaklands turn right again and at the end of Elmhurst turn left. On reaching some shops by a telephone box turn right down St Nicholas Road. At the top of this road there is an excellent view of the town across the river. Descend a long series of steps to meet the main road close to the Fox Inn and your starting point.

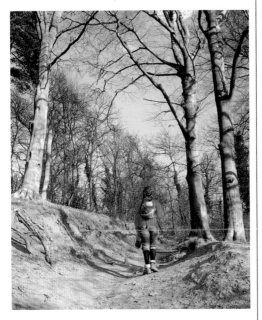

*Walker in
Hermitage Coppice*

Tourist information: The Library, Listley Street, Bridgnorth Tel: 01746 763257

WALK 3

Severn Up

Maps:	1:25,000 Explorer 218 Wyre Forest & Kidderminster Bridgnorth; 1:50,000 Landranger 138 Kidderminster & Wyre Forest area
Distance:	10½ miles approx
Car parking:	Low Town off A442 near Fox Inn (grid ref 721929)
Toilets:	Opposite Fox Inn and by Market Hall, Bridgnorth

Basic route: Bridgnorth, west bank of Severn upstream, Apley Bridge, Station House, Nordley, Astley Abbotts, Cross Lane Head, St Mary's Cottage, Cantern Brook, Bridgnorth

From the Low Town car park turn left, then left again to cross the River Severn. Turn right into Cartway and after a few yards take the road on the right and follow Riverside. The sandstone cliffs on the left are providing a secure home for birds, and sparrows are particularly active here. After a while the road narrows to become a track following the banks of the river, lined with willow trees.

Soon High Rock above the opposite bank comes fully into view, the impressive cliff face with its greening of Scots pine contrasting with the red sandstone as it rises almost sheer from the river with only just enough room for the road to make a way between river and cliff. After passing High Rock the path runs alongside the golf course and is soon passing the sandstone towers of Fort Pendlestone. From this low level route you have a different prospect of the high route explored in the last walk.

Long tailed tits are found in the trees that line the bank, perhaps visitors from the coniferous forest across the water. The River Worfe, the attractive river encountered in

the last
walk,
makes its
junction
with the
Severn on
the opposite
bank. At the end
of the golf course
cross a stile and con-
tinue along the river
bank. A feature of this
walk is the view of the high
wooded cliffs that wall in the
river on its east bank. The less

41

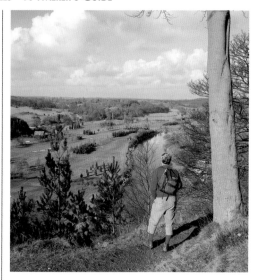

The low level walk upstream view from High Rock

than musical call of pheasants can be heard from the woods opposite.

Across the field to the left, and running parallel, is the low embankment of the now dismantled railway. On a winter's day in February we heard the melancholy sound of an owl calling across the river, not unlike the whistle of a locomotive, ghostly echoes of the past!

The fine but distant 'black and white' buildings to the left belong to Severn Hall. Across the river more caves can be seen cut into the cliffs near Winstone Cottage, beautifully sited high above the river. What a marvellous place this must be to live, particularly in the summer with a superb view of the valley of the Severn towards Bridgnorth.

The river curves slowly to the left with the high wooded cliffs of Apley Terrace across the water. As the railway embankment, path and river come together, early spring walkers will find snowdrops and primroses in sheltered spots. You may also see something slightly more unusual: cormorants, a surprise since they are normally

Apley Park

Apley Park was built by the Whitmore family early in the 19th century, in a superb position with commanding views of the river and the Shropshire landscape. The house passed on to the Fosters, who I understand were connected with the steel industry in Stourbridge. Recently it has seen service as a school and is now being renovated as a retirement home.

coastal residents, but now increasingly found around inland waters. Stately **Apley Park** comes into view.

Ahead lies the handsome white-painted **suspension bridge** ▶ that linked the Apley Park estate with the railway. It was built in 1905 by the then owner of Apley Park, and is still maintained in excellent condition, a splendid ornament to the river scene.

After passing under the bridge turn left and pass the old station house. Despite Mr Foster's generosity to his tenants, friends and employees, any such travellers today would have a disappointing wait. The last train ran in 1963 and the track was removed not long after. Indeed, but for the enterprise of the Severn Valley Railway Preservation Society the whole line would have been lost. Such is the success of their undertaking one can't help but wonder if one day they may be enabled to push the line north again from Bridgnorth.

Cross the old railway track and continue ahead. After passing through a five-barred gateway, the path is followed into a wood. After passing some cottages, continue forward, disregarding a path to the left. The way is never very far from a small stream. Ignore the first bridge on the left by a broken gate. About 100 yards after passing under power lines, cross the stream by a little bridge and go forward over marshy ground to join a muddy bridleway rising to meet a gate into wood. The path improves as height is gained.

When the edge of the wood is reached continue uphill with the wood to your left. When the trees fall back continue with a boundary fence to your left to meet the road by the Swan at Nordley, with its handsome inn sign. Turn left and follow the road (B4373) for just over

A notice on the **suspension bridge** reads: 'The bridge over the river is not open to the public but Mr Foster allows his tenants, their friends and his employees on their way to and from Linley station, to pass over the same, free of charge. All others must obtain permission'.

½ mile and turn left along a quiet lane when Colemore Green is signed. When a T-junction is reached, turn right to walk through the attractive village with the splendid ecclesiastically alliterative name of Astley Abbots. It's a tiny village with well maintained black and white half-timbered houses and a sandstone church. It still retains a Victorian post box, with the collection arrangements shown by the day rather than the hours.

Continue with the lane to reach the road (B4373) at Cross Lane Head, with its signpost of the old type carrying the name of the village within a circle in addition to directions elsewhere. It always seemed a good idea to tell people where they were as well as where they were going. Other versions of this type of sign carried the grid reference of its location, not nearly so useful for the general traveller. Nor is it hard to see how this settlement got its name.

Take the broad track opposite and follow it for a little over ¼ mile, just short of St Mary's Cottage. Here take a footpath on the left, over a waymarked stile to cross a field. (Note the path seems to follow a different course to

St Leonard's
Church, Bridgnorth –
a gunpowder store
in the Civil War

that shown on the map but the direction of travel is shown on waymarks on the stiles.) A second field is crossed diagonally right to its bottom corner. Cross a stile and ditch and follow the field boundary with Cantern Brook to your right.

At the end of the field meet a stile in a muddy corner and enter a wood. Continue forward on a rising and falling path with the brook sparkling and chattering to your right, another good habitat for birds. The path eventually descends to the brook to meet a bridge, which is crossed. Here take the route on the left, which climbs a stepped path to continue forward with garden fences on your right.

When an open grassy area in front of a housing estate is reached, continue forward to meet a path that runs along the edge of the wood to your left and again with garden fences to your right. A steeply wooded slope drops 100 feet to the brook and, among the plentiful population of birds, blue tits and great tits seem to outnumber the others.

The local museum is accommodated above **Northgate**, with a thousand or so items reflecting something of the town's past. Admission is free.

As the houses come to an end, the path descends with a wire fence to your right. Cross a stream by a plank bridge, then continue up a stepped path forward between a line of Scots pines, shortly meeting the road (B4373). At the road turn right to enter Bridgnorth by **Northgate ▶**, the only gate remaining of the five that once gave entrance, or forbade it, to the town

By the Golden Lion there is a mounting block, a relic of the days when the inn provided sustenance and accommodation for travellers who arrived on horseback or by the stage coach. After a short distance take the

St Leonard's Church
Whilst the church is no longer required for religious worship, it remains consecrated and is maintained by the Churches Conservation Trust. It was at this church the Royalists stored their powder kegs during the unhappy period of the Civil War, with disastrous results to the town and its people. This is a quiet spot reminiscent of the atmosphere of a cathedral close, if not quite on the same scale. Opening times: Summer daily 10–5pm. Winter Tue to Sat 11–3pm.

turning on the left which leads to **St Leonard's Church**, with its handsome sandstone tower.

In the close, for that is what I am tempted to call it, is a timber-framed house with a sign which reads: 'In this house lived the learned and eloquent Richard Baxter, 1640–1641'. How rewarding to be remembered as learned and eloquent, especially after such a short residence. It's all too easy to spend a lifetime in one spot and fail to leave a mark!

Richard Baxter, was a Presbyterian minister, who after a short stay in Bridgnorth worked in the carpet town of Kidderminster. During the Civil War he became a chaplain with the Parliamentarian army. His account of events and personal experience during this time has found its way into the histories of the period. He seems to have been an admirer of Cromwell, advocating his appointment as Lord Protector after the failure of the Commonwealth. Visitors to Kidderminster will find a handsome statue to Baxter outside the parish church.

Britain in bloom – Bridgnorth from the river

Opposite the church are the galleried alms houses of the Palmer's Hospital Charity, built in 1687. They were 'rebuilt and rendered more commodious, AD 1889, towards the cost of rebuilding, Mrs Colley, of Oldbury contributed £500', in those days a very generous donation that would have carried the work forward a long way. The original inscription, now fading, reads:

'ADMDCLXXXVII, these alms houses for 10 poor widows of this towne were built and endowed by Francis Palmer, the rector of Sandy in the County of Bedford who had an affection to this place (?), his mother being buried in this church and was sister to Colonel Francis Billingsley, late of Abbots Astley (???), slain in this churchyard in the service of Charles the First.'

A little beyond the Alms Houses is the narrow entrance to St Leonard's Steps, which, as a descent is made, offers views over the river to Hermitage Hill and upstream to High Rock. On reaching the road continue downwards by Cartway passing the Prince Charles Inn and Bishop Percy's house with the elaborate patterning of its timbers. At the foot of Cartway turn left to cross bridge and return to your starting point.

Tourist information: The Library, Listley Street, Bridgnorth Tel: 01746 763257

FEATURE 1
Bridgnorth – Sabrina Fair

Bridgnorth is a little gem. This old market town is full of interesting little lanes and alleys winding their way about the shops and its old inns. Many people visit the town just to enjoy the splendidly airy view from the Castle Walk. The sandstone on which Bridgnorth stands is easily worked and there are many caves that have been hollowed out of the rock. In Cartway a plate recalls that caves here were used as private dwellings up to 1856; there are similar caves beneath Castle Walk and elsewhere along the Severn Valley. A number are still in use today and you may encounter some garden sheds, a garage and even a house carved out of the living rock.

From Low Town, Castle Mount may be gained either by the Cliff Railway, installed in 1891, or by the Stoneway Steps... nearly 200 they say. Better still is to walk up the Cartway, following the age old route up to High Town. On the way, Bishop Percy's House is passed, arguably the most striking of the town's residences, a tall black and white half-timbered building dating back to 1580. Thomas Percy was born here in 1729, a scholarly man whose career in the church culminated in his appointment as Bishop of Dromore in Ireland. His publications included Reliques of English Poetry and Memoir of Goldsmith... he of She Stoops to Conquer and The Deserted Village fame.

Near the top of the Cartway lies the narrow Castle Walk running between old houses, one with the date 1665 cut into its timbers. As the houses fall back the river scene is laid out before the visitor. The view of High Town from the river is dominated by the handsome church of St Mary Magdalene, quite unlike the image of the usual parish church. It is beautifully proportioned; a square tower rises to support a clock with four faces above which a green dome is topped by a cross.

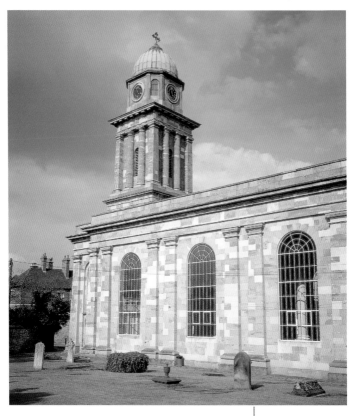

Within the church all is bright and airy, six great windows allow the light to come flooding in, a pleasant change from the gloomy darkness that is so often encountered in churches. Two rows of six columns each support the high roof. It is a place of dignity and peace but with perhaps more of the atmosphere of the concert hall than that of a place of worship, an impression heightened by the absence of plaques and memorials on the walls; in the context of this building a totally right decision.

Thomas Telford's fine church – St Mary's

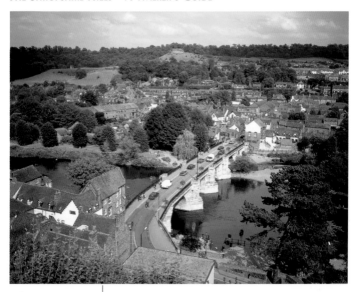

Bridgnorth – Low Town and River Severn from Castle Walk

It is a different church but then its architect was a man more famous in another field – that of civil engineering. He was none other than Thomas Telford whose list of achievements include the Menai Bridge, the Shrewsbury-to-Holyhead road and the Caledonian Canal. Telford originally trained as a stonemason before turning to the roads, bridges and canals for which he is best remembered. Had he continued with his architectural work how many more glorious buildings might he have left us today?

Behind the church is a tower, all that remains of Bridgnorth Castle, tilted at an impossible angle (17 degrees out of true). The town is built on an obviously important strategic position, commanding the roads and river. A burh, an Anglo-Saxon fortified town, was in being here early in the 10th century, with the Norman castle following after the Conquest.

Beyond the castle the view to the west takes in the railway station, and Pan Pudding Hill from which the bombardment of Bridgnorth was launched during the Civil War. The coming of the railway age made a major impact. The river had been an important source of trade and employment, bringing goods and customers to the long established market. The town was one of a number of inland ports along the Severn, the fast flow making for easy downstream progress, the upstream voyage dependent upon the muscle power of men and horses. There were coal and iron industries further downstream and the Bridgnorth wharves were kept busy with many kinds of traffic, until the rapid expansion of the railway network enabled the speedier movement of goods and passengers throughout the country.

The town was itself, in a way, responsible for the loss of the river trade, for just across the river at Low Town was Hazeldine's foundry. Two great names of the early railway age came together here. Richard Trevithick, the inventor of the high pressure steam engine, and the engineer John Rastrick. In 1808 Rastrick constructed from Trevithick's design the world's first passenger locomotive engine, the Catch me who can. Trevithick had a circular track laid in what is now Euston Square and demonstrated their joint achievement to the admiring citizenry of the capital.

To the north of Castle Mount is the main shopping area of the town, still with a number of attractive half-timbered buildings and the town hall dated 1652, its top half looking immeasurably better than its supporting bottom storey. Until about 1750 the assize courts for the area were held here. Strangely, it seems to have been acquired second-hand, the half-timbered part having served an earlier life as a barn at Much Wenlock.

Off the main street is St Leonard's Church, of which more later. Near here the Franciscan brothers established a Friary in 1245, which along with many greater religious houses, disappeared with the dissolution of the monasteries.

The Civil War is writ large in the histories of most Midland towns and villages for it was across this part of the country, as much as any, that the armies marched

51

Jubilee Gardens and the statue of Sabrina.

and fought in little local skirmishes or large scale set piece battles. Bridgnorth was no exception.

In the course of his manoeuvring across country and gathering his army together Charles I arrived in Bridgnorth in October 1642, apparently to a general welcome by the population. Whilst the King enjoyed the hospitality of Sir Thomas Whitmore within the castle, his army was accommodated in the town and the villages thereabouts. The King and the army soon moved on but during the course of the campaigning that flowed back and forth across the Midlands the castle came under artillery fire. Later, in March 1646, the Parliamentarian army successfully forced its way into the town. The Royalist defenders, following a scorched earth policy, started fires that led to the destruction of a large part of High Town, especially as powder kegs were stored in St Leonard's Church. More than 300 families were left homeless and without means of support.

We have touched a little upon the history of Bridgnorth. Meanwhile, if perhaps you are puzzled by the title of this chapter, Sabrina Fair, then I should explain that she is the goddess of the Severn. You will find her on Castle Mount, her charms enriching the small fountain acknowledging the life and work of Henry Whitmore – 'Faithful and valued representative of Bridgnorth in Parliament'.

Tourist information: The Library, Listley Street, Bridgnorth Tel: 01746 763257

For more information about places of interest in or near the town see Walk 1

WALK 4
Bewdley and the Wyre Forest

Maps:	1:25,000 Explorer 218 Wyre Forest & Kidderminster Bridgnorth; 1:50,000 Landranger 138 Kidderminster & Wyre Forest area
Distance:	8 miles approx
Car parking:	Dog Lane, Bewdley (grid ref 784754)
Toilets:	Close to car park, Bewdley
Note:	Part of this walk is on permissive rather than public footpaths – these are not open to the public on Christmas Day and New Year's Day

Basic route: Bewdley, west bank of Severn upstream, Dowles Brook, Wyre Forest – Knowles Mill, Park House, return by old railway track, Tanners Hill, Bewdley

This walk trespasses across the Shropshire border into neighbouring Worcestershire to explore the Wyre Forest. There are not many places where motorists can arrive and park their cars in the centre of the town and be off on their walking route in under a minute, but this is the case with Bewdley. Occupying an important position on the banks of the River Severn it has a satisfying long history having valuable connections with forestry, and the busy river traffic over many centuries.

This 8-mile walk starts from the Dog Lane car park, follows the river then pursues the course of Dowles Brook deep into the Wyre Forest. The forest, which covers some 6000 acres, lies to the west of the Severn and there is ample opportunity to enjoy the rich wild life of the mixed woodland, which includes deer and a wide variety of birds.

Across the river, a little beyond the eastern bank, you may see billowing smoke from the locomotives of the Severn Valley Railway, which keeps close company with the river for much of its 16-mile journey from Kidderminster to Bridgnorth. The fast flowing Severn has long been in use as a highway for the movement of

Coles Quay and the River Severn, Bewdley

goods and Bewdley was one of a number of towns that prospered as a port, further aided by the generous supplies of local timber for boat building and charcoal burning and the early bridging of the river.

From the car park head upstream. The riverside fringed with alders and pollarded willows is followed for about ¾ mile, until the tall brick pillars that once supported a railway bridge are seen ahead. Just before the pillars are reached, cross the footbridge over the Dowles Brook, turn left and in about 300 yards reach the road (B4194) and turn right. After a few yards pick up a path on the left which is found just beyond the old bridge abutments. The path edges a nature reserve and soon swings left to cross the brook. To the right can be seen the topiaried gardens of Dowles Manor whilst to the left is the steep embankment of a now disused loop line of the Severn Valley Railway.

About ¼ mile after leaving the road a broad track is reached. Here turn right. After a short distance the path divides, take the right fork which again crosses the brook. The picturesque Oak Cottage is passed, it is a delightful woodland hideaway, set under the trees with blue tits and coal tits very active around the garden.

These woods, particularly along the streams, are rich in **bird life**, but it is not only birds that will be seen and heard, the forest is home to a number of deer (400 has been suggested) and even if you miss seeing them, their

Bird life

Among the common birds to look for here are wagtails and dippers. At the time of our last visit we learnt that a heron had been fishing at the same spot on the Dowles Brook every day for weeks. The yaffling cry of the green woodpecker is almost certain to be heard and so will the harsh call of the jay. This colourful bird is an acorn eater and like the squirrel stores acorns for winter food. Spring should be a particularly rewarding time for the bird watcher, with the returning migratory birds likely to be more visible before being lost in the foliage of summer. A tawny owl may be heard, or a fleeting glimpse of a kingfisher caught as it darts along the stream.

slotted tracks on softer ground will confirm their presence. Squirrels abound, and despite efforts to keep them in check feral mink are thriving and no doubt taking their toll of fish and birds' eggs. Once crayfish could be found in the cool clear waters of the brook, but it is said that they have now been wiped out by a fungal infection.

Our route passes **Knowles Mill** ▶, it dates from at least 1757 and had a long working life, being in service up to the beginning of this century.

You may have seen a 'Danger – Adders' notice posted by English Nature. Local naturalists Sylvia Sheldon and Chris Bradley have been making a careful study of the snakes in the forest for several years. A count of adult adders in 1988 produced a tally of 205 over the entire Wyre Forest area. By the end of the century the numbers had dropped considerably. They think that perhaps there ought to be 'Danger – People' notice for the adder population. The snakes are quick to disappear when danger threatens and more often than not are on their way well before you have a chance to see them.

Do not cross the brook at Knowles Mill but continue, still with the stream to your left. About ½ mile from the mill the track turns left and crosses a stream. Once over the bridge turn sharp right and follow the line of a stream. Soon the path divides, ignore a left junction and go forward on the rising

Knowles Mill was purchased by the Cadbury family in the 1930s and presented to the National Trust. The nearby cottage is much older and has already passed its 400th birthday, certainly there is a written record of it in 1661.

Winter walking in the Wyre Forest

path looking down upon the brook. About ½ mile after the last crossing of the brook the path again returns to the other bank and swings left. After a short distance a forest road is reached, turn left along this and in about ¼ mile reach a ford. Just a few paces to the right from here you can cross dry shod by way of the footbridge.

The track now runs away from the river, climbing towards Park House and lined with elegant silver birches and young oaks. As Park House is reached, the line of the old railway is met running east to west. Turn left along this and follow it for nearly 2 miles. You'll alternate between the delightful prospects of the brook winding through the forest 200 feet below on one hand, being

Fishing in shallow waters – a dry summer at Bewdley

lost to the world in sheltered cuttings, and on the other side of the track catching glimpses of steep tree clad clefts with tiny streams glistening in the gullies.

As a gate just beyond a bridge is reached, a track leads off to Lodge Hill Farm; note the bat boxes on the trees to the left. Beyond the bridge the trackway is met-alled: continue with this until a T-junction is made with a narrow lane. Here turn right and follow it uphill between hedges, with improving views.

When a road junction is met, ignore Hop Pole Lane on the right and continue forward. At the summit houses are met. Here take the path signed off to the left. This descends over several fields, offering views of the Severn and the surrounding wooded hillsides. When you reach a metalled track by a house, turn right and meet the road (B4194).Turn right along the road, making your way back to Bewdley. Your starting point in Dog Lane is found in just over ¼ mile.

Tourist information: Bewdley Museum, Load Street, Bewdley Tel: 01299 404740

Bewdley Museum: Load Street. Open daily 11–5 Easter to end Oct

Bewdley Town Trail: Explore Bewdley with aid of the Town Trail leaflet, available from information centre

West Midland Safari Park: Spring Grove, Bewdley. Open daily Mar to Nov. Tel: 01299 400700 (recorded information)

Wyre Forest Centre: Callow Hill, on A456 west of Bewdley. Forest trail leaflet available. There are also car parks off B4194, north-west of Bewdley, which make good starting points for forest walks

FEATURE 2

Ironbridge

Shropshire explorers can no more exclude Ironbridge from their itinerary than the visitor to London can miss Westminster Abbey or the Tower. For here, rescued from dereliction and decay, is a complex of museums celebrating in a highly enjoyable manner the birthplace of the Industrial Revolution. To further underline its importance the Ironbridge Gorge became Britain's first World Heritage Site – a designation by Unesco that places it in a small but distinguished company.

Despite its great historical importance Ironbridge is also a unique family day out, though in truth you would be hard put to fully cover the area within the course of a single day. This has been recognised by the Museum Trust

The town from the Iron Bridge

which issues Passport Tickets that provide for admission on subsequent occasions to those museums that have not been visited – at the last count there were ten!

By far the best prospect of Ironbridge is found from the far bank of the Severn close to the Toll House. It is a convenient place to park a car and explore the immediate vicinity of the bridge. (Note: the various museums are spread over a wide area and it will eventually be necessary to move on.) The eye is carried across the river to the town as it rises in terraces above the river gorge. All now in excellent order, with houses in good English brick and a few in colourwashed render, with the church taking a prominent position opposite the bridge, the scene mildly suggesting a continental location rather than Shropshire.

The history of iron is a long one beginning, as far as this country is concerned, around 500 to 600 BC. The Romans took a hand in its manufacture as did some of the monastic institutions. Production methods developed slowly; water power came into use early in the 13th century and the blast furnace was in use by 1500. Iron was produced in many parts of the country, particularly where a plentiful supply of charcoal was available, such as the Forest of Dean and the Weald, where both limestone and ironstone were also found.

Iron had been made at Coalbrookdale from at least 1500 but it was the arrival of the Darby family early in the 18th century that expanded the industry in the area. Iron had become an increasingly important element in warfare but this was entirely alien to the Darbys who were Quakers and so they concentrated very successfully on the production of domestic items. The invention of the iron smelting process using coke instead of charcoal by Abraham Darby led to the cost effective production of iron in great quantities and heralded the Industrial Revolution. Seventy years later his grandson, Abraham Darby III was to use iron to bring about another revolution, this time in civil engineering with the construction of the world's first iron bridge.

The Iron Bridge was one of the wonders of its day – and still is

The Iron Bridge

The river which served for the transport of goods and passengers along much of its length was something of a hindrance to east–west traffic and the need for a substantial bridge had long been felt. Walkers exploring the Severn Valley today are still handicapped by the less than frequent provision of bridges, so the problems that confronted the architects and constructors of 200 years ago may be imagined. To bridge the Severn at this point was not easy, the sides of the gorge rose steeply from the river banks and adequate freeway had to be allowed for the passage of the considerable river traffic. A single span bridge seemed the answer if only the means to provide it could be found.

A consortium of local businessmen was formed to further the cause of bridging the river. Architect Thomas

Pritchard produced plans, Abraham Darby III took on the role of treasurer, as well as the responsibility for construction. The necessary Act of Parliament was passed in 1776 'for the building of a bridge across the River Severn from Benthall in the county of Salop to the opposite shore of Madley Wood, in the said county, and for the making of avenues or roads to and from the same'. There is no doubt that the project did not get under way without much deliberation and there must have been many misgivings. After all the builders were entering unknown territory. Work started in the winter of 1777, but it was not until New Year's Day 1781 that the world's first iron bridge was opened.

We may imagine that there was considerable cause for celebration at the successful spanning of the river and some statistics may not come amiss. The 24-feet wide bridge stands 40 feet above the river with a span of just over 100 feet. The toll house at the southern end of the bridge displays the original estimate of the cost of construction, £3200, which included the provision of 251

The Iron Men celebrate the Morris Dance on the Iron Bridge with their customary energy

tons of iron. In the event a further 100 tons of iron were needed so that the final cost of the project does not emerge. The bridge was private property and a toll was charged for the privilege of crossing the Severn. No one was exempt, a notice made that quite clear '… every officer or soldier, whether on duty or not is liable to pay a toll for passing over as well as any baggage wagon, mail coach or the Royal Family'. The bridge continued to produce a revenue until 1950 when the tolls were abolished. The charges will also be of interest. The table of tolls displayed includes upon its tariff: 'For every coach, landau, hearse, chaise chair or suchlike carriages drawn by six horses, mares, geldings or mules two shillings'. The rate for conveyances drawn by a single horse fell to sixpence. A cow could cross for a penny, a calf, pig, sheep or lamb, halfpenny as was a person on foot. There was also a charge for the use of the road (by those not actually making the crossing) at half the scale of the bridge crossing.

The visitor centre lies across the river and to the left, and features a history of the River Severn.

The Museum of Iron

The museum is housed in the former Great Warehouse and is next to the Coalbrookdale Company's foundry, with its tall chimneys still issuing smoke and proudly proclaiming the continuance of a long tradition in this special place.

The museum relates the story of iron from its earliest days, but it is of course with the products of Coalbrookdale and the ironmasters of the Darby and Reynolds family that it is especially concerned. As has already been mentioned the Darbys developed the domestic side of the industry and there is a collection of iron bellied pots ranging in size up to 400 gallons, of the sort that the comic strips illustrated as being used by cannibals to cook interfering missionaries. There are innumerable iron products from the really useful to the merely decorative. Ornamental hall stands, notices in cast iron favoured by the railway companies, a Victorian pillar box of 1870, and a host of fireplaces, pumps, mangles, cooking utensils, water closet cisterns, typewriters, seats, gates – the list is endless.

The construction of the Iron Bridge led to an increasing use of iron in many areas of engineering. The bridge had its supreme test and its value fully appreciated in 1795. In that year the volatile River Severn, swollen by heavy storms, lived up to its reputation and every bridge along its length sustained damage except one.

Thomas Telford, church architect and civil engineer made great use of iron. He designed the first major iron aqueduct on the Shrewsbury Canal. When he was entrusted with the construction of the Llangollen Canal it was iron that he used to make the thousand foot crossing of the Dee.

And so the story is unfolded from locomotives to lamp posts, sewing machines to suspension bridges, but one other set of firsts must be mentioned whilst leaving readers to make their own discoveries at the museum. It concerns that other great engineer with the splendid name, Isambard Kingdom Brunel, and a ship that was itself full of 'firsts'. Iron from Coalbrookdale was used to build the first iron ship, the SS *Great Britain*. Its launching at Bristol in 1844 gave the world not only the first iron ship, but the first propeller driven ship, the first iron buoyancy lifeboats, and the first ship with a bridge.

Clearly we have touched upon men of great stature and there is one other that is remembered in the museum but not in quite the same context of the word. He was William Ball, for 40 years a Coalbrookdale Company employee. His claim to fame was his enormous size. He turned the scales at over 40 stone, his other vital statistics including an 80 inch stomach, a 50 inch thigh and collar size 23½. It is recalled that when he went to the Great Exhibition in 1851 he was obliged to travel in the guard's van. He died the following year aged 57 and some 20 bearers were required to convey his mortal remains to his lasting resting place. His chair and walking stick survive to fill yet another interesting corner of the museum.

The Coalbrookdale Old Furnace, where Abraham Darby I pioneered the smelting process using coke in 1709 is preserved within a building a little away from the main museum. Here the noise and tumult is recalled in a small measure by a light and sound presentation, thankfully without the choking fumes and intense heat of the furnace. If Ironbridge was the birthplace of the Industrial Revolution then here is the womb in which it was conceived.

Rosehill

Only a short distance from the foundry is Rosehill, one of the Darby's family homes. Though they were wealthy people they lived close to the works, on call to deal with any crisis that might arise. Here an aura of peace and quiet prevails, though whether this is due to the careful restoration of the house, which was built in 1730 but now reflects the mid 19th century home, or the happiness engendered by its former residents, no one can say.

Amongst the many items of interest is the partners' desk where Abraham Darby III must have done much of his work on the Iron Bridge. A commonplace book with entries in a beautiful, highly legible copper plate puts most modern writers to shame. Few people can write like that today but even when Darby was still at school the exercise books shown in the museum demonstrate the firmness of hand and clarity of lettering that was a feature of the education of the day. As has been mentioned the Darbys were Quakers and there are a number of books including William Penns *No Cross, No Crown*, written in 1669, in an edition of 1750 and carrying the signature of Samuel Darby. Abraham Darby III's marriage to Rebecca Smith is well authenticated – the certificate being signed by no fewer than 65 witnesses!

Blists Hill Open Air Museum

If you are faced with the choice of only one of the museums to visit then this is the one that you can be sure all the family will enjoy. Here on a large site are a number of industrial and engineering wonders of their age intermingled with... 'a small town reconstructed showing how people lived and worked 100 years ago'. This has been a most successful excursion into the concept of the living museum. The staff wear the costume of the late Victorian period as they demonstrate the craftsmanship of the day.

To enter fully into the spirit you must first call at the bank and change your money into pre-decimal coinage specially minted for the museum. There is a huge pleasure in buying a cup of tea for a penny or a pint in the pub with its cosy fire.

You do not have to read myriad labels to find out what is going on – education or entertainment is effected by word of mouth. The chemist has his story to tell the crowds that throng his shop, with its enormous collection of bottles full of the mysteries of a past pharmacopoeia, and has a ready answer to any question. The candle maker explains the finer points of his trade and spices it with snippets such as the story of the pig that was kept in the sty next door and fed on the waste tallow.

Butchers, bakers, cobblers, printers, wheelwrights, brassfounders, locksmiths and more are there behind

The fierce glare of the blast furnaces brought visitors great distances to view the night sky. Turner came and recorded the spectacle in characteristic fashion

67

their counters or at their workplace to paint the picture in a highly practical and entertaining way of the life and times of everyman in Coalbrookdale and many another small town.

Blast furnaces, beam engines, mine shafts, pitheads with their winding gear and even a little gospel car made from an old tram is there, and more is being added. There is the comparative affluence of the doctor's house to be contrasted with the squatter's home, built within 24 hours, where a miner and his wife

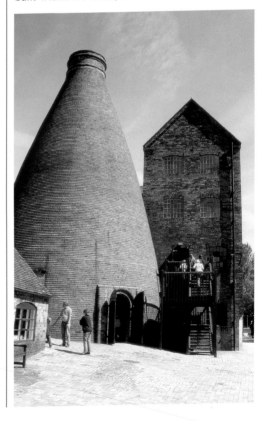

The great bottle kiln at the Coalport China Museum

brought up seven children in two rooms. The last of the trows, *The Spry*, a river craft unique to the Severn, has been restored here. It is not only children that are tempted to sit at the desks in the school room.

The museum is a mixture of the commonplace and the wonders of the age. In that last category must come the Hay Incline Plane, a marvel of inventive engineering that enabled barges to be moved up and down the steep sides of the gorge from the Shropshire Canal to the River Severn in a matter of minutes.

More and Yet Still More

Amongst the other museums and points of interest are the Bedlam Furnaces, the Jackfield Tile Museum, the Tar Tunnel and the Coalport China Museum.

Ironbridge achieved renown for its connection with many innovative projects; its museums can be proud of carrying on that tradition. The beauty of Ironbridge is the overriding excellence, not just into the history of its industry but in people who made it happen and those who worked for them at all levels. Here in this Shropshire riverside town is a microcosm of social and industrial history which changed the face of the world.

Tourist information: The Toll House, west side of bridge. Tel: 01952 884391

The museums are open daily 10–5 but check with tourist information for winter opening times. The attractions include: Blists Hill Victorian Town, Coalport China, Jackfield Tile Museum, the Tar Tunnel, Museum of the Gorge, Toll House and Iron Bridge, Museum of Iron, the Darby Houses, Enginuity and the Broseley Pipe Works.

WALK 5

The Wrekin Giants

Maps:	1:25,000 Explorer 242 Telford, Ironbridge & The Wrekin; 1:50,000 Landranger 127 Stafford & Telford
Distance:	5 miles approx
Car parking:	Close to start about 1½ miles north of Little Wenlock (grid ref 637093)
Toilets:	At eastern foot of The Wrekin

Basic route: The Forest Glen, south-eastern flank of The Wrekin, return over Little Hill and summit.

The Wrekin, 1335 feet, rises sharply from the surrounding countryside. At almost any weekend the car park is in full use as a fair number of people take a walk to the summit and back. Its popularity is related to the close proximity of Telford New Town and the tourist area of Ironbridge, coupled with its excellence as a view-point. Most of these visitors take the direct approach from the east and few of them find their way

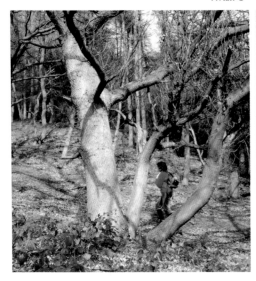

*Under The Wrekin –
a wooded approach*

beyond the summit. Whilst it unquestionably offers rewarding views for a relatively modest effort, it is not the best approach, the ascent from the west being more visually satisfying, with the Shropshire scenery gradually unrolling as the walk develops.

Take the steadily rising broad track opposite The Forest Glen, ignoring all paths to the right. Through the trees will be seen the steep face of the quarry by the car park, where the climbers practice their sport. A sharp elbow in the track marks a change in direction and ¼ mile from this the path turns sharp right for the direct approach to the summit. Resist this temptation and continue forward on a good track through the wood, immediately passing the collapsed remains of a building on your left.

The path is muddy in places, encouraged by slow trickles of water out of the steeply falling hillside. Birch and oak rise above the bracken and bramble on the floor of the forest. Gaps in the trees provide windows onto hills whose shapes have been re-sculptured by man's quest for their stone treasure.

The **nuthatch** is a small bird, about 5½ inches, that may be seen giddily descending a tree head first. Other regulars are the green woodpecker and great spotted woodpecker, both of whom nest in holes bored into tree trunks, at least one such nesting site is passed along the way. There are badgers, foxes and some seldom-seen deer, escapees from the National Trust's Attingham Park.

These wooded slopes provide a habitat for the usual woodland birds and **nuthatch** ◀ are found throughout the year.

Away to the left will be seen plumes of steam rising from the Buildwas Power Station, like huge pots on the hob about to boil over, giving modern credence to the story of the Wrekin giants. As the path advances there are glimpses of the Stretton Hills to the west. When the path divides, ignore left fork to the Shropshire County Scout Camp and go forward through Spout Lane and Little Hill Plantations to reach the road. Here turn right and after 200 yards re-enter the wood by a path on the right signed with the buzzard waymark of the Shropshire Way.

The path rises steadily through the conifers. Ignore all turnings to left and right. After a broad track is crossed the path steepens to climb to the summit of Little Hill.

The hillside has been cleared and replanted, giving excellent views for the time being from this comparatively modest height, crowned with a small clutch of Scots pines. From Little Hill, the digitalis lined path dips, gathering strength for the ascent through the trees to The Wrekin summit. The climb is as steep as many a mountain, and increasingly frequent pauses for breath give a tunnel's eye backward view thorough an avenue of trees to the Stretton Hills. At last the first view point at the western end of The Wrekin is reached. Here you are on top of the world, with the wind roaring in from the west battering the trees and threatening to dislodge you from your rocky perch. Beneath is the familiar pattern of pasture and plough divided by a network of hedgerows, one of the hallmarks of the English landscape. The tall cooling towers indicate the approach to Ironbridge, beyond the shapely towers the wooded hills rise sharply to make the western wall of the gorge. In the distance a great semi-circle of hills, Clee Hills, Long Mynd and the other Stretton heights. In the flat land ahead the Severn's meandering passage through the pastures is clearly seen, a silvered gleam quite unlike the muddy brown so often seen at closer quarters, before it is funnelled through the gorge.

In the far distance, at the outer edge of the circle, the grey blue smudge where sky and hills meet mingle into one and it is difficult to discern the difference between cloud and solid earth. Can you really see Snowdon on a clear day? It is a great place to watch the weather. On a fine day observe the gentle progress of high white clouds of summer trailing a veil of shadows upon the fields below. In winter, to willingly endure the wind's blast as the storm clouds come scudding across the Welsh borders, racing over the Long Mynd and Caer Caradoc, their heavy burden of snow pressed forward by an angry wind. In autumn to watch the sun shafting through the clouds, spot lighting varying features, a single farmhouse, the plumes of steam rising from the cooling towers, the crown of a distant hill, or its warming light bringing greater depths of colour to the trees and the browning of the bracken. All scenes from the theatre of the sky, adding to the richness of the landscape that makes all the year

A distant view to The Wrekin from Benthall Edge

The Needle's Eye

The story of how The Wrekin was formed is similar to ones related about other isolated hills. A giant (or the devil) is on his way with a great shovelful of earth to take his revenge on a nearby town – in this case, Shrewsbury. He meets a cobbler with a sackful of shoes which he has collected for repair. The giant asks the cobbler the way, and the wily cobbler tells him that he has already worn out all the shoes in the bag trying to find the way. The frustrated giant then dumps the earth, abandoning his intention to damn the Severn with a view to flooding Shrewsbury. Thus we have The Wrekin. Other versions of the story involve a fight between two giants who were building a home on The Wrekin. They fell out over the use of a shared spade, during the course of a violent argument the spade split the rock we now call the Needle's Eye, there's more, but enough is enough of tall stories!

round walking such a pleasure come rain, shine, or snow.

Just short of the summit a little path passes under the volcanic rocks that had their fiery creation 600 million years ago, a path that edges the steeply falling hillside.

The **Needle's Eye** is a cleft rock which legend says was split in twain at the instant of the crucifixion. How the dwellers here on the old hill top camp could possibly have known of the events in the Holy Land is never explained. Another story associated with the rock (and there are similar stories elsewhere) that a young lady taking the narrow passage through the eye was obliged to give her escort a kiss on emerging on the other side. Those thoughtless enough to look back would pay the penalty of never marrying.

The broad track over the summit passes through the western gate of the hillfort to arrive at the **topograph**

Summit Topograph

The pointer answers all those questions about distant landmarks. To the west, Caer Caradoc 12½ miles; Pole Bank Long Mynd, 16 miles; Devil's Chair on the Stiperstones, 17½ miles. Towards the north, the world's largest doric column honours Rowland Hill, Shrewsbury's famous general. To the north-west Snowdon, 71 miles; Berwyn Mountains, 37 miles. To the south the Malvern Hills, 40 miles, and more splendid walking with Clee Hill and Wenlock Edge 8 miles away, just to the west of south.

presented by the Wellington Rotary Club to commemorate the Queen's Silver Jubilee in 1977.

The biblical connection suggested by the Needle's Eye, is extended as the walker continues over the summit to pass through Heaven's Gate to descend a little (of course) before passing through Hell Gate.

There is a television mast tucked under the edge of the hill fort, a modern addition to the ancient home of the Cornovii. There is a firing range on the north of the hill, and the path is edged with a number of warning notices and flags. As height is lost the paths divide, take the path on the right. Cross a broad track, pass Wrekin Cottage to your right and continue with the broad track which winds steadily downhill to return to your starting point.

Tourist information: The Toll House, west side of bridge. Tel: 01952 884391

Attingham Park (National Trust): Stately Homes don't come much more stately than this. House open early March weekend afternoons from 1pm. Late March to end of October daily from 1pm except Wed and Thurs. Grounds open daily.

Benthall Manor (National Trust): Open April–June, Tues/Wed 2pm. July–Sept also Sundays.

Wroxeter Roman City (English Heritage): Open daily from 10am but not Mon/Tues Nov–Feb.

FEATURE 3
Much Wenlock

Much Wenlock is a delightful little town that has not out-
grown its strength and newer housing in the area has not
diminished the heritage of the past. The modest size of
the town makes practical an exploration of its places of
interest in combination with some of the walks described
in this book.

Much Wenlock is a mixture of half timbering, limestone
and brick, and since many of the old properties are in
very good order, the town repays a gentle stroll. Some of
the buildings have been 'labelled' by the local historical
society and interesting reading they make. Ashfield Hall
for example, is believed to be the site of 'St John's
Hospital in the 13th century for lost and naked beg-
gars...' it has served as an inn, a private residence and
offered hospitality to Charles I during the Civil War when
he was on passage from Shrewsbury to his Oxford head-
quarters. A particularly careful restoration has been
made on the beautifully timber-framed home of John and
Mary Raynalds which bears their name and the date
1682. Barclays Bank is housed in a black and white
building that was once the Falcon Inn and there are other
fine old inns still continuing in business.
　　The many arched and jettied Guildhall dates from
1540 with later additions and its handsome upper storey
is still used for the Magistrates' Court. Its lower floor
served as a corn market, with livestock being brought
into the town each Monday. The town's history as a trading centre dates back to the early part of the 13th century
and probably much earlier. Trade and pilgrims would
have been attracted by the presence of the religious
foundations, as indeed is the modern day tourist. It must
have been a busy market centre for a notice of 1850
warns of the penalty that might be expected by any
thoughtless enough to obstruct the way – a sort of 19th-
century parking ticket. 'Waggoners and others, Notice is

Raynalds House

The Guildhall – from the east

hereby given that under the 34th bylaw in force in the Borough of Wenlock every person who shall on any Monday being market day between the hours of nine o'clock in the morning and six o'clock in the evening drive any waggon or cart, empty or laden with coals, stone, lime or bricks or other materials, such waggon or cart not being used for the purpose of taking goods to or from Much Wenlock market through, along Smith Street or such part of High Street that lies between Spittle Street and the Fox Inn in the town of Much Wenlock in the said Borough shall be liable to a penalty of not more than £5 or less than one shilling for every offence, and such fine will be strictly enforced from and after the day of this notice by order of the Mayor. R. C. Blakeway Town Clerk 16th Sept 1850'.

The borough's minute book records some of the costs associated with the building. Paid to Richard Dawley for building the court house, £13.6.8. and paid to Edward Brook for the belfry with lead, 14 shillings and 4 pence. Paid for the carriage of shingles to the court house 1/6d. Paid for wine to the various men for reward 4 shillings and 9 pence – it must have been quite a celebration!

Wenlock Priory

The priory owes its origins to a Mercian King, Merewalk, who placed his daughter Milburgha in charge as Abbess in AD 682. Quite how she came to be canonized does not fully emerge, quite possibly sainthood came more easily in those distant days, but she seems to have achieved considerable popularity and her name crops up elsewhere in the county. Under her guidance – a period that lasted some 30 years – the foundation flourished and popular legend credited her with miraculous works. She was buried within her priory and in later years a shrine was built to which the usual crop of pilgrims came to make their devotions or look for benefits.

A well, still to be seen in the town, carries the saint's name and water from it was once said to cure eye diseases. Many other wells elsewhere, at Malvern for example, have a similar reputation and perhaps the waters did have soothing qualities. Another piece of folklore associated with the well extended into the 19th century. It took place on the Thursday in Holy Week when the unattached young ladies of the town would meet at the well in the hope of ending their single state. It was their custom to throw bent pins into the well, at the same time wishing for the man of their dreams to make an early appearance. Meanwhile, the young men who might be expected to be the answer to these maidenly desires

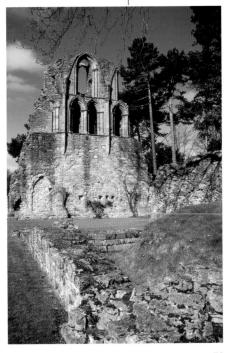

Wenlock Priory

79

would have been encountered swigging beer brewed from rain water which had been collected from the church roof. The logic of all this escapes me, but that is no reason to spoil a good story!

There is nothing to be seen of Milburgha's original priory. It was succeeded by a Cluniac foundation. The priory remains that we visit today were the work of Prior Humbert during the first half of the 13th century. The prior was a confidante of Henry III and was entrusted with various diplomatic missions both overseas and with the neighbouring Welsh. The dissolution of the monasteries put an end to Wenlock Abbey as it did for many others. Not that the monks were badly treated, in common with other such institutions their adherents were found places in the church elsewhere or pensioned off with not ungenerous settlements.

Today only the birds remain to sing evensong where the several religious communities performed the offices of the day. Despite the dereliction following the reformation the site is still impressive and it is not difficult to imagine it as it was in days of its glory. An artist's impression of the priory can be seen in the town's museum which adds flesh to the bare bones of its present skeleton.

The Parish Church

The church can claim a history dating from c AD 680 when it was built for the nuns of the abbey. The foundation's first Abbess, Milburgha, was buried in the Lady Chapel. Her bones and coffin came to light in 1101 and were moved to the newly built Norman priory. The nave was the work of the Cluniac monks about 1150 but the sporting enthusiast may be expected to take rather more interest in the memorial to Dr William Penny Brookes, whose story is told in the local museum.

Much Wenlock Museum

Amongst the many exhibits giving the flavour of the town's history is a display devoted to the good Dr Brookes and detailing the formation of the Wenlock Olympian Society, which from then on provided a field of athletic competition which attracted attention beyond the bounds of the small Shropshire town. So much so that Brookes is credited by some as being the true architect of the revival of the Olympic Games. Certainly it was the big event of the year in the Wenlock area. The 27th meeting in 1877 offered a first prize of £5 for flat tilting, £1 for pole leaping and the successful competitor in a 200 yard race for boys aged under 14 received 5 shillings. The victor in a 3-mile bicycle race could claim £5 and tilting at the ring on horses over two flights of hurdles was handsomely rewarded with a prize of £10.

Old photographs of the games reveal that they were taken very seriously indeed. The spirit of Merrie England was about and the champion tilter is shown with his herald standing by a tournament tent in the style apparently favoured by the medieval jousters. This was no rough and ready knock about to please the village on an autumn afternoon; the participants turned out in appropriate dress and the herald is shown in the costume of his calling of the 16th century, with maroon cape, fine shirt, handsome boots and topped off by a plumed hat. The pentathlon was one of the events and it seems the games founder was a considerable competitor in his own right. A painting shows him with the pentathlon blue riband and an olive crown.

Tourist information: The Museum, High Street, Much Wenlock Tel: 01952 727679. Same times as for museum. Contact Bridgnorth at other times.

Museum: Daily opening from April to October, with occasional opening during the winter Tel: 01952 727679

Guildhall: Open all year; Sundays afternoons only

Wenlock Priory (English Heritage): Open May to August daily. Mar–Apr and Sept–Oct: Wed–Sun. Nov–Feb: Thurs–Sun

WALK 6

Wenlock Edge and the Desperate Rider

Maps:	1:25 00 Explorer 217 The Long Mynd & Wenlock Edge and a tiny fraction of Explorer 242 Telford, Ironbridge & The Wrekin; 1:50,000 Landranger 138 Kidderminster & Wyre Forest area
Distance:	5½ miles approx
Car parking:	National Trust car park B4371, off A458 (grid ref 613996)
Toilets:	Much Wenlock
Note:	Reference is made to coloured way-mark posts – beware of changes – they do not necessarily follow our route and should only be regarded in conjunction with the text.

The long legged and stout-hearted may be tempted to walk the Edge end to end, from **Much Wenlock to Craven Arms**. Subject to appropriate transport or accommodation being arranged it is both a practical and appealing prospect. In this connection YHA members will be aware of the hostel at Wilderhope Manor.

Basic route: Much Wenlock NT car park, Blakeway Hollow, Major's Leap, Blakeway Coppice, Harley Wood, Stokes Barn.

When walkers come to Wenlock Edge they are in Housman Country, so evocatively recalled in *A Shropshire Lad*, published in 1896. Housman writes of the hills, the little towns and the rivers which we are exploring and as Elgar walked the Malvern Hills and found the inspiration for some of his great music, surely Housman found the magic of his words upon The Wrekin, along the Edge, or reflected in the silvered waters of Severn, Teme or Corve.

Wenlock Edge, as narrow as its name suggests, runs for some 15 miles between **Much Wenlock and Craven Arms** ◀, its limestone spine the legacy of the time, hundreds of millions of years ago, when warm tropical seas washed over this countryside. Small parties who are able

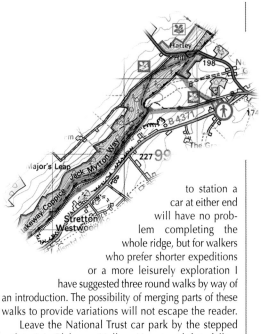

to station a
car at either end
will have no prob-
lem completing the
whole ridge, but for walkers
who prefer shorter expeditions
or a more leisurely exploration I
have suggested three round walks by way of
an introduction. The possibility of merging parts of these
walks to provide variations will not escape the reader.

Leave the National Trust car park by the stepped
path to join Blakeway Hollow. Here turn left to follow
this wide track, the relic of an old road, rising steadily
with improving views. From time to time remains of old
lime kilns will be seen. These kilns were used to reduce
the limestone to agriculturally useable lime. The way is
edged by now overgrown drystone walls, so often an
indicator of good walking country.

A twin ridge is seen to the left, its green banks rising
swiftly from the scoop of the dale, while to the north-east
the tree clad Wrekin imposes its presence upon the scene.

As the summit of the lane is reached the path
divides, take the left fork which passes through a six
barred gate. Soon on the left a white waymarked sign
points the direction of Major's Leap. This path follows
the inside edge of the wood, with ramson, that pungent
flower of the woodland, beginning to show through in

Major's Leap
It was here, the story goes, that Major Smallman of Wilderhope Manor, made a legendary escape. During the Civil War, as a Royalist he found himself the fox in a life or death pursuit; the pack that followed him were the supporters of the Parliamentary cause. The hunters were gaining fast upon him and the cliff-like slopes of Wenlock Edge were before him. Escape seemed quite impossible, but he urged his mount forward into one last death defying leap off the high edge. Incredibly, although his horse was killed beneath him, the Major survived to limp away, borrow another horse and make fully good his escape! The 'leap' is marked by a small seat. Here the trees fall back a little allowing views to the Long Mynd and the Stretton Hills. An excellent place to pause and enjoy the landscape. The quarries have made substantial inroads and here the edge is perhaps not too far from having disappeared altogether; a reminder of the fragile environment in which we live.

spring. Shortly a stepped path carries the walker a little higher to follow a narrow path with steep slopes to the right and glimpses of the landscape through the trees, somewhat more visible in winter than when summer leaf jealously hides it from view. A bridle path parallels our way on the outer edge of the wood and above the quarries. From here the stratified layers of stone are clearly seen, composed of the skeletons of countless billions of sea creatures, whose fossilised remains continue to be found.

Ahead Brown Clee Hill is seen, a winter's powdering of snow gives it a resemblance to a Christmas pudding topped with white sauce, a radio mast doing duty as a holly sprig, completing this fanciful illusion. **Major's Leap** is reached in ½ mile from the signpost.

From Major's Leap continue forward on the outside edge of the wood; beech, ash and some Scots pine. Brown Clee Hill achieves increasing prominence until the eyes and ears are distracted by the rattle of machinery and the roar of dumper trucks as the main quarry buildings are neared. When you draw level with these buildings, albeit situated beneath you on the quarry floor, the path comes to an abrupt end. At this point take the path signed off to the right to Presthope.

Descend the hillside on a narrow path to reach a broad track. The route to the left will eventually lead to a further car park at Presthope, ignore this and turn right to return on a parallel course signposted 'Much Wenlock, 2 miles'. Soon a couple of seats placed with a view forward to Blakeway Farm and the dale beyond allow the opportunity for comfortable refreshment. When the path divides, ignore the left fork and continue forward, soon to pass under Major's Leap, where Smallman, the Evel Knievel of his day, made his prodigious jump.

Continue forward ignoring the small stepped path on the right that would return you to the Leap. As the edge of the wood is reached the outward route is joined for a few yards. Just beyond the gate take a path on the left signed to Harley Bank. Follow a wide path that curves to the right to descend through the trees giving

Walker on Wenlock Edge contemplates Major Smallman's prodigious escape

occasional glimpses of the long line of the Edge running off to the west.

When the path divides ignore turn to the right and continue until a gateway is reached at the edge of the wood, which gives onto a broad way. Here The Wrekin is seen boldly ahead. Do not join the parallel track on the left but continue forward on the track which rises through a conifer plantation. The Jenny Wind Incline which carried limestone to the kilns crosses the track, and the Shrewsbury road is seen through the cleared ground that accommodated its passage. Continue forward with a stand of tall and slender birch trees to the left and The Wrekin showing through the lattice work of their trailing twigs.

A disused railway line makes for easy walking – and a wild flower haven

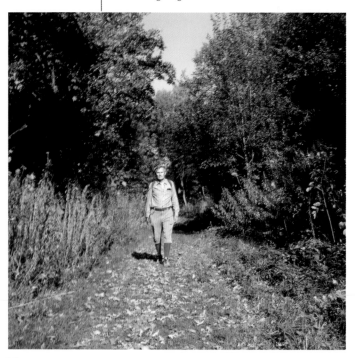

Soon the grey waymarked route is rejoined to continue forward with the Shrewsbury Road again seen at the foot of a steep bank. At the top of the rise, turn right, signed 'Much Wenlock ¾ mile'. The bank on the right is sheltered, catching the sun for most of the day. The primroses flower early here, a welcome sign of spring for the regular walker.

The path climbs steadily, passing a badger's sett and giving improving views over the plain towards Shrewsbury and to the great bulk of The Wrekin when cleared spaces allow. The path dips a little before climbing a stepped path. Just beyond the top of the steps, take the path signed Much Wenlock to pass through a gate and follow the left hand edge of a field towards the limestone buildings at Stokes Barn with its impressively large doors. The evidence of former quarrying in the fields suggests the possibility that the buildings were constructed from materials found on site.

Just beyond the house swing off to the right to meet a waymark post. A short field is crossed to pass through a gate and take a descending path over a field, which leads to a stile. Here turn left into Blakeway Hollow and, after a few steps, turn right over the stile to return to the car park.

Tourist information: The Museum, High Street, Much Wenlock Tel: 01952 727679

For more information please see Feature 3 (above)

WALK 7
Ippikin's Rock and Spring Lamb

Maps:	1:25,000 Explorer 217 The Long Mynd & Wenlock Edge; 1:50,000 Landranger 137 Ludlow & Church Stretton or Landranger 138 Kidderminster & Wyre Forest area
Distance:	5 miles approx
Car parking:	National Trust car park, Presthope B4371 south-west of Much Wenlock (grid ref 582975)
Toilets:	Much Wenlock

Basic route: Presthope, Ippikin's Rock, Easthope Wood, Easthope, Natal Coppice, Dove Plantation, Presthope.

From the car park take the wide, signposted bridleway which descends through the woods, passing some venerable yew trees. After about 100 yards the path divides, here turn left. This is something of a wild flower walk; in spring primroses edge the track and wood anemones, another herald of spring, are seen in profusion. At the foot of the hill, turn left along a lane which runs along the edge of the wood to reach and cross the Hughley road.

*Taking a breather
on Ippikin's Rock –
a robbers' hideout*

Take the path opposite to climb through the woods; a glance back will reveal the great bulk of The Wrekin. Another favourite spring flower, the little violet, is found just off the path as well as an occasional celandine. After about 150 yards a stile gives onto the broad track of an old railway. Here turn right and then immediately left to take the uphill path signed to Ippikin's Rock. The woodlands have an undercover of wild flowers, some rather distant from the path, but nevertheless seen brightly through the trees.

The path rises and falls, but ignore all turnings, maintaining your direction by reference to the green arrowed waymarks until Ippikin's Rock is signed by a stout post. A short uphill pitch is lined with ramsons. Having walked quietly and alone through the woods it is a minor surprise to find the summit may already be occupied.

Ippikin's Rock is close to the road and the Wenlock Edge Inn and in consequence is a stopping place on the tourist route. First the view, then the legend. The views that have so far been denied to you are now revealed as you stand on the edge of this rocky observation post, looking beyond the steeply falling, tree covered Edge to the green dale, still well hedged and with a haphazard scatter of farms. The Stretton Hills fill the left horizon

Ippikin's Rock

Ippikin cannot be cast in the same mould as the dashing Major Smallman, in fact, he appears to have been no more than a common criminal. Legend has it that he was the leader of a band of thieves who hid themselves and their ill-gotten gains in a cave beneath the rock. Justice seems to have triumphed in the end when a fall of rock sealed the cave and brought a not undeserved conclusion to their criminal careers.

while away to the right The Wrekin will be seen – a sweeping view, not overly dramatic, but the cliché 'green and pleasant land' springs to the mind.

The village to the north is Hughley which has achieved a perverse sort of fame owing to Housman's poetic licence in conveniently amending the architecture of its church: he changed its tower to a steeple in order to rhyme with people! Actually, he gets the best of both worlds by calling it a tower a few lines on.

Having enjoyed the view, and possibly the hospitality of the inn, retrace your steps to the original path just below the rock. Here turn left and after a short distance make a junction (no pun intended) with the old railway track and turn left with it.

Just after crossing a bridge over a lane you'll encounter a 'Private Woods – Please Do Not Trespass' sign. The railway track is abandoned. Take the lane uphill to meet and cross the B4371, taking the road opposite signed to **Easthope.** Brown Clee Hill shows up a little mistily and violets and wood anemones are found on the

Easthope

Easthope is a small, peaceful village lying beneath the Edge, with a mix of half-timbered and stone buildings. It is a delightful place to be in the spring when lambing is in full swing with the farmyards turned into maternity wards for the new arrivals. The young lambs are full of fun and are soon on their feet and out in the fields, running pell mell in little groups, or playing king of the castle on any small mound that will serve the purpose. Sheep cover the opposite hillside, looking like a distant fleet of sailing ships upon a sea of green. Think not of mint sauce at a time like this.

banks of the lane. From the village take the lane signed to Much Wenlock and after 300 yards take the wide track on the right to make a rather circuitous return to Presthope on the waymarked paths of the Shropshire Way.

At end of the first field pass through a metal gateway as the path bears right and head to a gateway opposite which carries the buzzard waymark. Once through the gate bear half left across the field with Natal Coppice to your right. An arrow on a telegraph post points the way, the path following the outside edge of the coppice. As the coppice falls back head for the opposite field boundary to cross a stile by an ancient oak in a corner of the field. Go forward on a hedged path to emerge into an open field. Here turn left to follow the field edge down a slope towards Dove Plantation. A stile is crossed to follow the short edge of the plantation to a further stile and gate, reached in about a 100 yards.

Once over the stile go forward for a short distance with a hedge to the left. Just before a pond is reached, a waymark on an old stump by a metal gate directs you right, to cross a field to pass a second pond on your right, then to meet and follow a field edge with a fence on the left. Shortly after passing a gateway (do not go through) join the hedged track ahead, which whilst once wide enough for farm carts, is now somewhat obstructed by brambles and the like.

After emerging from a mild battle with the forces of nature, the path heads diagonally, roughly north-east to a metal gate and to join a track. After a short distance this merges with a quarry road, but the path soon goes forward (on the right) to join the road. Here turn left to ascend to the B4371. Turn right at the junction, passing the quarry works with its great stacks of neatly cut stone ready for delivery. After a short distance the car park that was the starting point of this walk is seen ahead.

Tourist information: The Museum, High Street, Much Wenlock Tel: 01952 727679

WALK 8
Hope Dale and the Edge

Maps:	1:25,000 Explorer 217 The Long Mynd & Wenlock Edge; 1:50,000 Landranger 137 Ludlow & Church Stretton or Landranger 138 Kidderminster & Wyre Forest area
Distance:	8½ miles from Easthope cross roads or 4 miles from Wilderhope Manor
Car parking:	For start of walk from Easthope crossroads (grid ref 561955) but parking in the vicinity is not advisable. There is now a public car park and toilets at the National Trust's Wilderhope Manor so motorists are recommended to pick up the shorter walk (Route A) from that point (grid ref 545928)

At the crossroads on Wenlock Edge

Basic route: Easthope, Lutwyche, Pilgrim's Lane, Wenlock Edge, Wilderhope, Lower Stanway, Hopes Cross, Stanway Coppice, Wrensnest, Pilgrim Cottage, Easthope.

This is the last of the Wenlock Edge walks scheduled for this book, although it will be clear from a study of the map that there is further good walking in the area with many paths and tracks on or near the Edge. These include sections of the Jack Mytton Way (bridle paths) and the Marches Way.

Main walk from Easthope: From the crossroads head downhill towards Easthope. After about 300 yards take the path on the right through a metal gate to follow a broad track with a farm to your left. After passing a handsome house on the left, pass through an iron gate and follow the waymark, heading for Lutwyche Hall seen ahead. The route follows an indistinct track to the right of a broken line of trees. When a further gate is seen ignore this and continue forward with a wire fence to your right.

As a large dutch barn is reached, pass through a metal gate, which carries a yellow arrow and the buzzard sign of the Shropshire Way, and turn immediately left on a broad track to pass **Lutwyche Hall** on your right.

From the Hall there is a good stretch of walking along a broad straight track to reach Pilgrim Cottage. It is clearly an old building and should have a story attached to its name. Locally it is believed to be associated with another row of cottages on the Edge, now gone, whose occupants together with those of Pilgrim Cottage took passage on the Mayflower to the New World in search of the religious freedom denied them in their home country.

Lutwyche Hall

It is a handsome building but one that suffered a tragedy and many years' work have been devoted to the restoration of the east wing after a fire early in 1989. The Hall is in the best tradition of the English country house, enhancing the beautiful setting in which it was built. Mellowed brick towers rise either side of the south entrance with high mullioned windows topped with balconies balancing the towers. The house looks across the dale to the heights of the Mogg Forest, the highest point of which accommodates an old hill fort.

In spring these **woods** are full of bluebells, wood anemones, and primroses are to be found with other wild flowers to follow in season.

At the cottage turn right up a narrow lane and continue to the wood at the top. Here turn left with the dark recesses of the **wood** ◀ on your right. After a short distance a five barred gate is met and from hereon the path follows the outside edge of the wood with views opening up here and there through the gaps in the trees to give a sight across Ape Dale and with the lumps and bumps of the Stretton Hills forward right.

The little settlement of Longville in the Dale is seen to the right.

Three fields are crossed along the wood edge until a covered reservoir topped by a small weather vane is seen. Here turn left and head downhill towards Wilderhope Manor. The Manor, which had hitherto been out of sight, soon comes into view with its tall chimneys and projecting rounded stair well, a patina of dignified age apparent upon its lichen roof and mellowed stone walls. Owned by the National Trust, it is a youth hostel, and whilst now furnished to fulfil that function is nevertheless open to the public on two afternoons a week (see information box at end of walk). This was the home of the gallant Major Smallman, an officer in the Royalist army who made his death-defying leap further up Wenlock Edge and whose story has already been related. Dating from the 16th century it is a stone fortress of a house, a place apparently in need of a sturdy protection – not the least perhaps for its residents. But then these were troubled times. One of the interesting features is a great rack above the fireplace in the dining hall which once held 13 bows; now only five arrows remain of this armament store.

Main walk contd and start from Wilderhope Manor (Route A): From the Manor cross the waymarked stile, with 'Corve Dale' incised into its timbers, to continue on the Shropshire Way to Lower Stanway and Hopes Cross. Follow the broad track to pass farm buildings and, at a division of paths indicated by two stiles, take the left choice – still with the broad track. The path curves with the boundary hedge on your right to pass a clump of trees in an area known as The Bog. At the end of the wood cross a plank bridge and turn half left to follow a wire fence on the left with a stream beyond. At the field corner, cross a waymarked stile and go immediately left and over another plank bridge, then right to follow the stream edge. Jump a few small ditches, then a stile gives onto a lane at Lower Stanway.

Turn right over bridge and in a few paces turn left over a stile to follow the stream on your left. At the end of a short field cross a further stile, then a small stone bridge, turning right to follow the stream.

Continue with the path through the fields, resisting all temptations to cross the stream, however inviting the little bridges may seem. Eventually Brown Clee Hill is seen ahead making the southern backcloth to the scene. As Hopes Cross is neared a small row of cottages is seen on your left, cross the track which leads to them and go forward to a waymarked stile and through the remains of an old orchard. After a short distance swing left through a gap in the hedge. We now start the return leg of the walk, following the great curve of the Stanway Coppice which rides the long ridge above Corve Dale.

Make your way uphill keeping to the outside of the coppice from which the heady scent of bluebells escapes in the spring and with glimpses through the trees down to the valley along which you have just travelled. At the end of the first large field, pass through a metal gateway and continue on a broad track passing an old quarry, now very obviously a dumping ground for the unwanted. As height is gained the tops of the Stretton Hills are seen gradually gaining prominence.

Beyond the summit the wood falls away, but continue forward along the line of the hedge to meet the bottom edge of the plantation. Here pass through a gate on your left and head diagonally right over the field to meet and pass through a gateway by a giant ash tree. This is a good spot for a photograph looking down the valley towards the distant Fegg Farm. Beyond the gate to the right is Wrensnest, delightfully, if remotely situated.

Follow the edge of field with the boundary to your right. As the path drops steadily downhill, Wilderhope Manor can be seen away to the left, set under the wooded Edge. Cross a stile and go left to follow boundaries to join the broad track of the Shropshire Way. The pool in the next field, not shown on some maps, has become a favourite spot for wildfowl. If returning to Wilderhope turn left to reach the car park in about 300 yards (**Route A**).

Easthope Church

It has had something of a chequered history. It has the distinction of still retaining the hour glass which used to measure the length if not the value of the parson's sermon. It is housed in a wooden case dated 1662, bearing the initials of SS – Samuel Steadman. Whether it was his idea to measure his performance, making sure he gave full measure, or whether it was there at the suggestion of his long suffering flock who felt that an hour was quite long enough, thank you, does not transpire. The churchyard contains the tombs of two monks of Wenlock Abbey who murdered each other during a drunken fight at the manor house. An earlier incumbent murdered his Patron, John Esthope, in 1333 and his ghost is reputed to have haunted the churchyard ever since. Church was never like this in my younger days, and perhaps you should be cautious about speaking to any unfashionably dressed strangers you may encounter in this area, especially if cowled or cloaked. It comes as no surprise that somehow the building was burnt down in 1928, cause unknown, speculation invited.

Main walk contd: Turn right with the Shropshire Way and in ½ mile turn right again and then left at Pilgrim Cottage to return to the road on the route of your outward journey. Turn left to the cross roads. The little **church at Easthope**, with its squat tower, is seen ahead on the return.

Tourist information: The Museum, High Street, Much Wenlock Tel: 01952 727679

Wilderhope Manor: Owned by the National Trust but used as a youth hostel. Open 2–4.30 Wed and Sun Apr–Sep, Sun only Oct–Mar

WALK 9

The Stiperstones

Maps:	1:25000 Explorer 216 Welshpool & Montgomery; 1:50,000 Landranger 126 Shrewsbury & Oswestry and Landranger 137 Ludlow & Church Stretton
Distance:	7 miles approx
Car parking:	2 miles north-west of Bridges on the right of the road under eastern side of Cranberry Rocks (grid ref 369976)

Basic route: Cranberry Rocks along ridge to Shepherd's Rock, Perkins Beach, Stiperstones village, Snailbeach (edge of) Crowsnest, Castle Ring fort, Blakemoor Flat Old Tips, Shepherd's Rock, Gattan Plantation

The Stiperstones is a 3-mile long ridge bisected by a narrow winding road. The southern half is mainly forested but the northern section is high, bare moorland rising to 1758 feet, with rocky outcrops adding drama to the landscape. It forms part of a National Nature Reserve covering some 1100 acres with information boards at a number of points. More detailed background is also to be found on the western side of the hill in the area known as The Bog, once a small mining community, from which further expeditions can be started. It is a remote area, not far from the Welsh border, as will be noted from the title of the 1:25,000 Explorer map. Some directions may be helpful to the motorist in finding the starting point of the walk. Leave the A49 at Church Stretton and, after passing through the town centre, take Burway Road, which makes a spectacular climb high above the Carding Mill Valley to the top of the Long Mynd. When the road divides take the right-hand branch signed to Ratlinghope and an equally exciting descent, if you have only just learned to drive. Continue to Bridges and on to the eastern edge of the Stiperstones ridge where a large car park is found – shown on the OS maps.

From the car park head up the wide grassy track and, as height is gained, take the path diagonally left to visit Cranberry Rocks, one of a series of rocky outcrops, reminiscent of the Dartmoor tors, which erupt spine like along the ridge, adding greatly to the dramatic quality of the landscape. The upper slopes of the ridge are heather covered and the going rough in places with shattered quartz-like rock littering the peaty way over the tops. The rock glints in the sun setting needle sharp points of light winking at your feet. A mild scramble will take you to the top of the rocks to survey the view. To the west is Wales, Corndon Hill large on the skyline is actually across the border in Powys. Behind it Offa's Dyke makes its long journey up the length of the border country, and beyond lies the former county town of Montgomery.

To the east the great rolling ridge of the Long Mynd fills the view with its highest point on Pole Bank, and as progress is made along the ridge, The Wrekin will be seen to the north-east. The valleys provide pasture for sheep and cattle, the upper slopes are wild moorland, or dark forest. Grouse make a swift, low clattering flight if disturbed, kestrels hover ever on the look out for their prey and buzzards soar and glide with an ease that is the envy of earthbound man.

A wild country to be enjoyed and respected, here the air is rarely still and in the winter, (and many another time) the wind blasts across the tops with a cutting edge that is Sheffield sharp and walkers that

A little on the wild side the Stiperstones – Manstone Rock looking towards the Devil's Chair

have not had regard to the provision of an extra pullover may soon regret their carelessness.

From Cranberry Rocks, head northwards along the ridge towards Manstone Rock, at 1758 feet the ridge's highest point. It is an exhilarating walk at any time of the year, although this is no place to set a cracking pace, for the sharp pointed rocks are a bar to speed, and in winter frequent icy spots make it doubly unwise. Like me, and many others before, you will look for the shape that might suggest how the rock got its name, from a distance it looks obvious, but the man proves to be the triangulation point and we must look again, and maybe come to no strong conclusion. There is a sphinx-like outline of a head that is my best candidate so far but I am not convinced. It must join a long list of similar rocks that are eagles, lions, a man playing an organ or whatever, which imagination and the right light have perpetuated.

On then to the **Devil's Chair** a great curve of rock that is rather more believable in its shape than

The Devil's Chair

The Devil's Chair gets its name from a mix of local legends. One is that Old Nick was carrying a great bundle of stones in his apron for some nefarious purpose and that, having rested on the ridge, his apron gave way and scattered the stones. Another story has it that the Devil was determined to destroy the bible-reading people of this country and believed that if the Stiperstones disappeared back into the bowels of the earth England and all its God -fearing citizens would be destroyed. The great weight of stones along the ridge is offered as proof of his attempt to bring about our destruction.

Manstone. Another invitation beckons to a better view from the extra feet gained from the top, only a minor challenge to scramble up from the western side but rather more tricky on the eastern face. It has of course the usual crop of folklore, legend and fantasy, put to good use in Mary Webb's *Gone to Earth*, a pleasing Victorian drama turned into a film in which the young Jennifer Jones starred many years ago.

Legend says that those troubled by having to make a difficult decision, find a solution here. It was necessary to come up here at midnight and dance three times round the Chair and if the sound of the Devil's **music** ▶ was heard, the answer to a question was yes.

This is a sparsely populated area with just a few farms to be seen scattered across the wide landscape, and out of sight from the top there is a handful of houses tucked under the shelter of the hills. Now much more thinly peopled than in the past, this area once supported a thriving mining community centred in the area known as The Bog. All that remains now is the Field Studies Centre, which in previous existences has served as chapel and local school. The search for nature's buried treasure, mainly lead and barytes, has left its mark and the walker will encounter spoil heaps, abandoned shafts and long disused engine houses along the way.

As if all this talk of the Devil is not enough, witches too come onto the scene, for it is on the highest point of the **Stiperstones** – that is Manstone Rock, not the Chair – that they were reputed to gather each year to elect a leader.

Continue onward along the ridge towards the pyramid shape of Shepherd's Rock, just short of which a large cairn marks a crossing point of paths, an especially helpful indicator to the winter walker when snow may disguise the way. Here we turn left to make a drop into the valley, ahead is the blue grey smudge of the Welsh hills. Soon the path loses height, a respite is found from the wind and the surrounding hills close in upon the walker. There are traces of the former mining activities in ruined buildings, shafts, old paths and rail inclines with,

Always there is the **music** of the wind to be heard, sometimes soft, sometimes loud – no wonder there were those who could be persuaded that they had indeed heard the music. Dancing over this treacherous terrain at midnight is a sufficiently hazardous occupation by itself without inviting the intervention of the Devil to take a hand in one's private affairs. Certainly there is a price to pay for such foolishness and in Mary Webb's novel, Hazel the heroine falls to her death down one of the abandoned mine shafts whilst trying to protect her pet fox from the hunt. Gone to earth with a fearful vengeance.

Stiperstones – another legend

There is a story dating back to the 11th century concerning Edric, very much a local hero who, lost on one stormy night on the Stiperstones, chanced upon a house filled with beautiful young women. Bewitched by their music he falls in love with one of their number and takes her away to be his wife. She is no ordinary young girl and warns him never to question her absences from home, when presumably she is off visiting her sisters. As in all good legends the day comes when, exasperated by her absence, he demands an explanation. The lady, of course, vanishes for ever, leaving Edric to a melancholy death. There are other legends connected with 'Wild Edric' the huntsman who still haunts these hills, and all in all it is clear that we must have a care when we pass this way!

here and there, a spoil heap. None of this is intrusive, nature is a master at reclaiming its own, and the work is well advanced.

The scenery is magnificent with the steeply sloped hills coloured in pastel shades of green, brown and yellow to your right. To the left, often without the benefit of the sun's kindly illumination to bring it to life, the hills stand blackly, with just a suggestion of menace about them adding to the atmosphere of the walk.

The Stiperstones – descending to Perkins Beach

The path bears off to the right, soon to meet a descending path to the left. Continue your downhill progress passing spoil heaps. It is one of those descents where you are glad to be going down rather than toiling up, for looking back the ridge above looks like hard work to gain. The signs of current habitation appear and the track is soon running between houses. A curve in the path brings into view the sharp, almost vertical drop and outline of Oak Hill and Blakemoor Flat.

The Methodist church of Perkins Beach is passed and soon the road is reached with the Stiperstones Inn just a few yards to the left for those who feel in need of its hospitality. There is a path that runs under Oak Hill, parallel with the road, but it is narrow and not user friendly to those in shorts and sleeveless shirts. To avoid this little local difficulty, turn right and follow the road for about ¾ mile to reach a sign which announces the edge of Snailbeach. Here on the left is a **former mine building**, still with its tall chimney ▶, which has been converted into a private residence.

The road bends sharply here and at the foot of a short hill take the narrow lane on the right, at first with a few houses on either side and then quickly rising up the narrow wooded valley. The path keeps company with a small stream, with steep hills on either side, and a similar barrier ahead blocking the way and suggesting the need for a considerable expenditure of energy.

The buildings are soon left behind, a gateway is negotiated and, after passing a green caravan of uncertain age, a further gate. Continue forward on the broad, still rising track and about 300 yards from the last gate ford the stream, soon to pass a remote stone cottage on the left. Continue onwards and upwards, passing a nature reserve sign. A narrow path leads up to the summit on which Castle Ring, the old hill fort stands. Resist the temptation for the moment and continue forward towards the summit of Blakemoor Flat. When this is neared an easier approach can be made for those wishing to inspect the fort. As height is gained a streamlet is crossed, the path narrows and there is a short soggy

I had been watching the process of the transformation of the **former mining building** chimney on various walking trips and had the pleasure of a chat with its resourceful owner. There were many problems to overcome, not the least the 500-foot deep mine shaft in what is now his garden, now safely filled in and capped with concrete. It seems that the shaft failed to come up to expectations and was abandoned without producing any great return. The old boiler, dated 1860, has been sandblasted, painted black, the great round doors through which the fuel was shovelled making a unique pair of cupboards and no doubt a talking point at dinner parties.

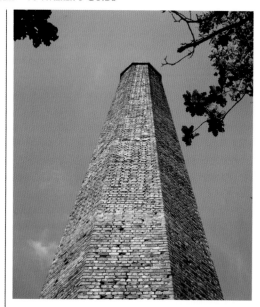

The Stiperstones has centuries of mining history – the chimney at the lead mines museum, Snailbeach

section. A crossing path by a pair of firebeaters, just short of the summit, takes you right towards the fort area. In truth there is not a lot to see although no doubt a trained archaeologist would think differently.

Having taken a look at the Ring, resume your course for Blakemoor Flat. From the top a dramatic outline may be seen ahead, the misty and mysterious Devil's Chair, its appearance fully in keeping with all the old tales. As the path reaches the saddle, a narrow crossing path is met coming off Blakemoor Flat, turn left with this and head up towards the ridge not far from the edge of a steep drop to the scooped out valley to your right.

When a crossing path running north–south is reached, about 100 feet under the top of the ridge, turn right and follow it as it terraces the hillside. It is a narrow but clearly defined path through the heather giving superb views. On reaching the bare open ground of the spoil tips, at the eastern end of the 1443-feet high Green

Hill, go forward a few yards and continue with the terraced path, again running below the top of the ridge. As progress is made Green Hill falls back and there is a view down the route of our earlier descent to Stiperstones village. Again the Devil's Chair makes an impressive appearance upon the eye, at this distance and angle, more so than at closer quarters.

The path curves easterly above the valley head, still a little under the ridge, passing between gorse bushes and gaining height. Soon the top of Shepherd's Rock comes into view. A short wet patch is crossed, heading towards the rocky outcrop to the south, and then the broad track from Shepherd's Rock is joined. Turn left with this to meet the cairn encountered on your outward journey.

A choice of return routes is available. You can follow your outward journey back along the ridge with its mysterious silhouettes of the rock outcrops, or take the southeasterly track from the cairn. This heads towards The Hollies, a steadily falling path giving excellent views to the Long Mynd. When the National Nature Reserve is reached, pass through a gate and maintain your direction. After passing through a gate with the buzzard waymark sign, continue half right, downhill to meet a broader track. Here turn right and after a few yards bear right, as waymarked, to cross a stream. After a short distance a muddy track becomes apparent. Follow this through Gatten Plantation. At the end of the plantation continue forward to return to the car park in just over ¼ mile.

Tourist information: Church Street, Church Stretton Tel: 01694 723133

Snailbeach Lead Mines: Interpretive panels explain key aspects of the site. Tours may be arranged through Shropshire Mines Trust.

WALK 10

The Long Mynd – Carding Mill Valley Circuit

Maps:	1:25,000 Explorer 217 The Long Mynd & Wenlock Edge; 1:50,000 Landranger 137 Ludlow & Church Stretton
Distance:	5½ miles approx
Car parking:	Carding Mill Valley (grid ref 447 943) National Trust members free
Toilets:	Carding Mill Valley and Church Stretton
Caution:	This route has a steep descent to return to the Carding Mill Valley and in common with other high level routes should only be under-taken in clear weather

Basic route: Carding Mill Valley, Motts Road, Wildmoor Pool, north-eastern flank of Haddon Hill, Bodbury Ring

The Long Mynd is the crown jewel of the Shropshire Hills and thankfully a large area of it is in the care of the National Trust which has the protection of this valued landscape at heart and a concern for the interests of walkers and riders. Clear waymarking at many points are of great assistance to walkers, how-ever good their map reading abilities may be. It should be noted that not all of the paths that criss-cross these hills and valleys appear upon the map and navigators need to bear this in mind. Some of the paths are no more than sheep tracks and may peter out but others are well used.

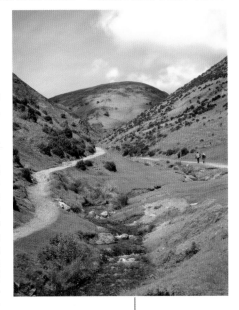

The key to exploring the area is the valleys (batches or hollows as they are called locally) that thrust deep into the Mynd following the course of little streams and leading the walker up to the high moorland plateau. Despite the sug-gestion of a long moun-

Carding Mill Valley

tain inherent in its name, the Long Mynd is moorland, and in fact, as the National Trust points out in its excel-lent descriptive leaflet, the most southern grouse moor in the country. Although it has to be said you don't see too many grouse these days.

The Mynd and its batches make excellent year-round walking but despite the civilising appearance of the lower Carding Mill Valley, the walker is setting out into upland terrain, which weather conditions can ren-der unfriendly, and on occasion positively hostile. The usual precautions for upland walking should be observed, particularly in uncertain weather conditions where snow, low cloud, or failing light may make navi-gational skills rather more important than a gentle stroll on a summer's day demands.

This and the next two walks will serve as an introduc-tion to the delights of the Long Mynd, whilst in no way pretending to be an exhaustive survey of the area. Walkers

Carding Mill Valley

The constant flow of water off the hills ensured that a mill had been kept busy in the valley for perhaps 1000 years, although initially it was not for the processing of wool but for corn grinding. The carding mill (which combed the wool ready for spinning) served the needs of local spinners from early in the 19th century. Later the enterprise was extended to include weaving and spinning, but it was never the large industry that we associate with the woollen towns and the buildings had several changes of use. The National Trust's shop window displays one of the last blankets made here at the beginning of the 20th century.

who follow these routes and note the destinations of the various paths that cross their way will soon be planning further and longer excursions, including trips over the Mynd to the western side visiting Darnford, Ratlinghope or Medlicott for example.

Carding Mill Valley receives many visitors and for some it will be their first introduction to hill walking. On a summer weekend the extensive car parks are likely to be filled to near capacity, but despite the large number of people who arrive in the valley only a fraction venture much out of sight of the vehicle that brought them. So if you prefer to walk in comparative solitude, don't despair, most of the others will be left behind within a few minutes, and the vast acres of the Long Mynd will quickly absorb the rest and leave you pretty much to your own devices. Whilst you may be anxious to be on your way and reserving a visit to the Trust's premises for one of their famous cups of tea after your walk, it is worth while taking note of the news sheet which is issued freshly each month detailing the wildlife likely to be seen.

From the car park take the path which runs up the valley thrusting its way deep into the Long Mynd, with interesting offshoots up minor batches that hold the promise of further expeditions away from the main tracks. At the final car park the road gives out and a stream is crossed by a little plank bridge. Make your way forward with the stream on your right and the hills folded in great dips, down which many nameless watercourses tumble and intriguingly a score of paths.

With the car parks and buildings left behind the walker is in a world of steep hillsides terraced by winding paths and narrow sheep walks. Despite the sharpness of the slopes that swoop down into the valley the westward paths gain height steadily making for comfortable walking along clear ways. Grassy slopes are mixed with patches of bracken and stunted trees manage to maintain a precarious foothold before the upper slopes and summit are given over to a wide expanse of heather – glorious in August!

The Reservoir – Carding Mill Valley

Ignore all temptations to take paths to the left or the right, despite their obvious attractions and continue up the main valley. The path narrows, with the occasional rock step to negotiate as the walker follows Mott's Road, named after a local doctor whose practice must have taken him over these hills on many a bright day or dark night.

A look back down the track reveals Church Stretton between the great V cut-outs of the hills but that apart, most signs of today's civilisation are left behind and young adventurers may begin to imagine they have wandered into a remoter world than the map would suggest. Indeed, a film producer on a modest budget might conveniently locate this as the Khyber Pass, or a highland glen for some epic of the Jacobite rebellion.

As the top of the valley gives way to the rolling plateau the path divides. Take the left fork. Before moving on pause to take another look back to the elliptical curves of the hilltops before they plunge steeply into the valley with Church Stretton seen hazily to the east, beyond which another range of hills close in. As the way flattens out onto the moorland those making a return pilgrimage to these hills after some years absence may be disappointed to find that the once familiar sight of the tent like shape of the Shooting Box no longer comes into view. It was always a good navigational reference and is still signed on marker posts and maps.

Soon a direction post is met where three paths run close together. They signal Pole Bank to the left, High Park to the right, but our way lies ahead to Wildmoor Pool. Whilst many of the, sometimes unmapped, paths over the Mynd have widened and come into more regular use, this crossing of Wild Moor is less visible and it may be preferable to use the alternative shown after the Wildmoor Pool detail.

Route via Wildmoor Pool

Cross the tracks and head a little west of north over the moor on a wide path which soon changes character, narrowing to the width of a single tread but still clear, even if the heather brushes against bare legs. The long spiny ridge of the Stiperstones makes the western horizon, and in a dip in the moorland, Wildmoor Pool can e seen at a bend in the road.

The path takes the walker to the road by the pool, with a small slightly soggy area to be crossed before the hard metal is underfoot. This is a lonely place sitting in the bottom of a shallow bowl in the hills, cut off from the world except for a single track road. The moors stretch for miles, almost to reach out to join the high banked clouds that fill the sky. The hollow is a natural collecting ground for the waters of the moor and the pool having

Wildmoor Pool

gathered together the blessing from above, sends it on its way in the direction of Darnford by a stream with the unattractive name of Colliersford Gutter. I recall being here on a still day when almost the only sound to be heard was the croaking of amorous frogs.

From the pool follow the road eastwards for just over ½ mile (ie turn right at the junction of the path with the road). A signpost to Woolaston and Ratlinghope is passed with the road curving to the left to reach a small semi-formal car park area on the right a little short of a cattle grid. A plantation to the left will help identify the spot.

Alternative Route Missing Wildmoor Pool
Take the broad track to your right; it is clearly marked on the map. Follow it northeastwards for about half a mile to meet the minor road and forward to the semi-formal car park area mentioned above and continue as below.

From here the route will cross high moorland with spectacular **views** ▶ to make a junction with the western edge of the golf course near Bodbury Ring as follows. There is a confusion of paths here but from the car park go forward on a narrow tread through a broad grassy area (direction at first is a little south of east). After a short distance the paths divide, take the right fork. After a further short distance a crossing track is met, go over this and forward on a narrower but still grassy way falling between bracken.

When a junction is made with a second wide crossing track turn right with this for about 400 yards, rising gently. Keep a sharp lookout for a small stone cairn where turn left. You will quickly identify the path, for within a short distance it passes two small springs on your left – the little blue eyes of the hills. The general direction is now south-easterly (with about 1000 yards to be covered to reach the path which drops down to the golf course). From the springs there is a clear way through bracken and some heather as it heads along the flanks of Haddon Hill.

As the golf course eventually comes into view and then disappears, keep forward. The golf course soon

Improving **views** are unveiled across a wide sweep of the eastern arc. The Wrekin, The Lawley and Caer Caradoc are easily identified to which is added the long wooded slopes of Wenlock Edge. Then Brown Clee and Titterstone Clee Hills are seen and, as progress is made, in the far distance the dark profile of the 9-mile run of the Malvern Hills – best seen just before the descent to the golf course.

reappears. Bear left with a curving, descending path with the golf course becoming more prominent. As the way starts to bear right turn left descending steeply on an initially narrow path through bracken with the western boundary of the golf course seen below.

Head towards the tall white post that marks the position of one of the greens and turn right keeping the fence line on your left until you can join the narrow but distinct path that curves uphill to Bodbury Ring fort. As you pass between Haddon Hill and Bodbury Ring there is a fine if restricted view of the Carding Mill Valley, increasing the impression that this a little Switzerland.

The path to Bodbury Ring is a narrow sheep walk terracing the hillside and giving quite magnificent views with the streams trickling down the hills sparkling in the sunlight. Burway Road is identified as it makes its tortuous way over the Mynd by the tiny cars grinding their way slowly along its steep edge.

When the ring is reached turn left, eastwards, across the fort area, but before continuing on your way take a circuit of this high hill fort, a very defensible area, and offering superb views, especially of the hills that run along the eastern side of the A49, The Lawley, Caer Caradoc, Helmeth and, beyond, the curving heights of Hope Bowdler Hill running on into Wilstone Hill.

The path from the Ring falls steeply towards, but not to pass through, a wicket gate in the golf course fencing. When this is reached swing right down the deep cleft to return to the Carding Mill Valley and your starting point.

Tourist information: Church Street, Church Stretton Tel: 01694 723133

Carding Mill Valley National Trust shop, café and information: Open daily Mar–Oct and winter weekends. Car park open throughout year

Stokesay Castle (English Heritage): Craven Arms. Open May–Aug daily. Mar–Apr, Sept–Oct: Wed–Sun. Nov–Feb: Thurs–Sun.

Acton Scot Working Farm: Open daily except Mondays. From 10am end of March to end of October and Bank Holiday Mondays. Tel: 01694 781306

WALK 11

The Long Mynd – Ashes Hollow and Pole Bank

Maps:	1:25,000 Explorer 217 The Long Mynd & Wenlock Edge; 1:50,000 Landranger 137 Ludlow & Church Stretton
Distance:	6 miles approx
Car parking:	Informal parking (grid ref 441919) – see text for detail
Toilets:	None close at hand, nearest Church Stretton

Basic route: Little Stretton, Ashes Hollow, Boiling Well, Pole Bank, Round Hill (edge) Cross Dyke, edge of Callow, Little Stretton

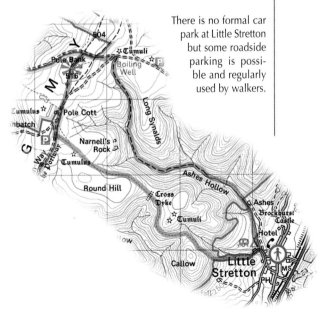

There is no formal car park at Little Stretton but some roadside parking is possible and regularly used by walkers.

Thatched church at Little Stretton

If travelling from Church Stretton take the first turn on the right-hand side past the Ragleth Inn and at the end of the lane turn right again, where it is the custom for cars to be left along a streamside.

Little Stretton is an attractive small village with several interesting features, in particular the 'black and white' thatched **church of All Saints**.

All Saints' Church

This is not an ancient church, but one that originated in the early part of the 20th century. The memorial tablet inside the church explains . 'This church was built in 1903 for Alice Elizabeth Gibbon of the Manor House… for more than thirty years she devoted her life to the people of Little Stretton. Beloved in the village she carried comfort and happiness wherever she went. Her life was an inspiration to all who knew her. Died Feb 19 1932'. There can be relatively few people to whom such words can be honestly applied. The roof was once of corrugated iron, but the replacement by thatch is a great improvement. The interior of the church is panelled throughout in wood and even the font is wood faced. Clearly the church is still carefully looked after and on a recent visit we noted the beautifully embroidered altar cloth, with a crown and roses against a cream background.

Opposite the church is the Ancient House, dating from 1516 and close by the church is the long, handsome half-timbered Manor House. Set beneath the timeless hills of the Long Mynd, the village itself gets scant mention in the guide books and its bypassing by the main road has served to preserve its air of peace. The lack of a car park does not encourage casual visitors to linger and those who come by intent are here because of the quite superb walking. The route described in this chapter is my own firm favourite of all the Shropshire Hills, although the Stiperstones runs it a close second.

Take the lane that runs behind the Ragleth Inn and after, passing Brook House, turn left over the footbridge to cross a stile on the right signed to Ashes Hollow. The path passes through a camping and caravan site with the stream to your right. It should be noted that this stream is followed throughout the first section of the walk to meet the road at Boiling Well. There are, however, several tributaries and it is not impossible to branch off on the wrong route, thus ensuring some confusion. Checking the incoming valleys and their streams should avoid this little problem.

Winter scene – the path to Boiling Well

At the top of the campsite, cross a stile by a sign which says 'Private property, footpath only', and continue forward, still with the stream to your right.

At the end of the long valley field, cross the National Trust estate boundary. In a few yards the path meets a rock wall and is diverted over a plank bridge by Ashes. From here head up the valley on a wide clear path. Ashes Hollow is quite different in character from the Carding Mill Valley, with a personality of its own that somehow seems softer and kinder, although the enclosing hills are just as steep. To the right are the slopes of Ashlet, then Yearlet and to the left, Nills and Grindle.

The path keeps close company with the stream, in truth there is nowhere else for it to go, sometimes crossing and recrossing from bank to bank. As progress is made other batches run into the main valley, each with narrow paths running alongside the streams, offering opportunities for further exploration on little paths, many not shown on the map. This is an invitation that can be accepted as experience of the topography is gained. Later on in this walk we shall look down upon part of our outward route, giving a better impression of how it

Looking into the depths of Ashes Hollow

fits into the jigsaw of the landscape than is gained from the restricted views of these lower levels.

Further up the valley the stream has to be paddled across; a good opportunity to test the waterproof quality of your boots. At one point the valley narrows dramatically, so that the walker is hemmed into what for want of a better word is best described as a gutter. The hills rise steeply from the notch with room only for the stream and barely room for the path. I wonder if the path totally disappears at this point after an exceptionally heavy storm or a fast thaw following a bad winter.

Certainly there is no problem of wayfinding, you are channelled into the only possible route. At the end of the narrow gully, the stream divides and so do the paths. Take the left fork to follow at times a twisting, winding track in sympathy with the stream as it comes tumbling fresh and clear down the hillside. After a few steps the opposite bank must be followed for a few yards before returning to the right-hand bank. (This will confirm that you are on route.)

Again the steep sides of the hills close in to squeeze the walker, almost vicelike, in the bottom V of the valley with, now and again, a little scramble to assist progress. Soon the brief but enjoyable rough and tumble gives way to a narrow, clear and easily walked track with the valley opening out, but still deep in the womb of the hills and with a restricted horizon which is bounded by the encircling hills.

Above the rim of this tiny world the silent planes of the Midland Gliding Club soar high, offering humans something of the freedom of the birds of the air. As the valley opens out, the slopes of the hills are seen to be covered with a mix of grass, bracken and heather with the ubiquitous stumpy hawthorn getting a foothold where it can.

Remain with the clear path that has the stream to your left and, as you progress more northerly, ignore all diversions along other streams. The stream and the walker arrive at its source, Boiling Well, close to the road. It is well named, a squelchy area with a scummy top like a great green jam pan. More than one sheep has injudiciously set foot here and has passed the point of no return as sometimes evidenced by the sad sight of a sodden woolly carcass half submerged in the spring. But walkers are in no danger, for a clear path alongside takes them dry shod to the road.

Now we are out on the high rolling moorland plateau, with boundaries of the horizon rolled back, even The Wrekin can be seen, peeping chad like over the top of the moors to the north-east. Little tracks through the heather are trail-blazed by untidy strands of wool, combed out of the sheep as they passed by.

At Boiling Well the now familiar square post waymark directs you to Pole Bank. Follow a broad track through the great carpet of heather. The rising and falling contours of the moorland must be a surveyor's nightmare, with the land crinkled, folded and rolling out in many curves wherever you look.

At the top of the rise the long ridge of the Stiperstones comes into view, its lower slopes green pastures whilst the darker colours of the forest plantations and blackness of the heather delineate the higher ground. Corndon Hill, pimple pointed at one end, is seen just across the Welsh border. Pole Bank is achieved by a left turn on a broad track guarded by two posts designed to keep vehicles off the top and soon the walker is on the **summit of the Long Mynd**, 1692 feet above sea level and promising great views.

Summit of the Long Mynd

A toposcope celebrating the diamond jubilee of the founding of the Council for the Protection of Rural England in 1986 directs the eye to distant peaks that are only too often obscured by heat haze, low rain clouds or mist. Despite the assistance of the many pointed toposcope is it possible to have set eyes upon the great bulk of Cader Idris? Snowdon, 101km distant, is denied to us, Plynlimmon 70km, perhaps not – and is that grey smudge the Malvern Hills? We must be content with the certainties of nearer hills, The Wrekin, Caer Caradoc, and the Stiperstones.

*The heather-clad
summit of the
Long Mynd*

From the summit continue on the wide path to meet the road, crossing en route the Port Way. This is an ancient track running over the Long Mynd, said to date as far back as the Bronze Age, which suggests its use for 4000 years. Certainly it is an old trade route. It is not a name exclusive to these hills, many Port Ways crop up on the map, indicative of an old way leading to a market town rather than a harbour.

On reaching the road turn right, passing the protective square of trees surrounding the former Pole Cottage, and watch for the path signed on the left to Little Stretton, which is reached in about 400 yards from the cottage site. From here a generally south-easterly direction is followed for over 2 miles to make a return to Little Stretton, a high level route that is scenically very rewarding.

Heather moorland ▶ has a special character, which the Long Mynd shares with parts of the North York Moors National Park, sections of the Pennines or parts of Dartmoor and Exmoor.

At first the return route to Little Stretton pursues a broad and rutted track along the plateau, passing the twin summits of Round Hill to your right. Take care not

Here in midweek there are few people around and you may tread a quiet and lonely track with the breeze whispering through the **heather**. When a hazy sky defeats the sun's efforts to fully light the landscape the subdued tones become almost colourless until the vast carpet of heather blooms and the moors come into their days of glory.

119

to be diverted when the track swings to the right, curving towards Round Hill, but keep forward on a narrow track, which passes along the flank of the next hill and which soon broadens.

After a while the land on your left falls steeply down to the Ashes Hollow route and your outward path can clearly be seen winding through the valley over 400 feet below. The path swings a little to the right, pulling away from the edge, and dips briefly before rising to pass through a break in Cross Dyke, to run high above Barrister's Batch and Callow Hollow, each with its blue veined stream. The wide track is easy to follow with no temptations to stray off on misleading paths.

The path dips a little as the huge mound of Callow is approached but passed on your right. Soon Little Stretton is seen ahead and beyond the sharp pointed southern end of Ragleth Hill. The path passes beneath the summit of Callow on the right and above Small Batch on the left. The terraced way opens up to give a long prospect of the hills keeping company with the A49. When a fence is met maintain direction, keeping it to your right and dipping down towards the stream below with its short row of willows. Pass through a five-barred gate and go forward, soon to ford the stream and join a lane by the campsite, close to your starting point.

Tourist information: Church Street, Church Stretton Tel: 01694 723133 and at National Trust shop Carding Mill Valley

WALK 12
The Long Mynd –
Minton and the Packhorse Way

Maps:	1:25,000 Explorer 217 The Long Mynd & Wenlock Edge; 1:50,000 Landranger 137 Ludlow & Church Stretton
Distance:	5 miles approx
Car parking:	None in Minton, but see opening text for alternative start; for walk start from Minton (grid ref 431906)
Toilets:	Nearest in Church Stretton
Note:	A bus shuttle service operates on summer weekends – Church Stretton, All Stretton and the Long Mynd summit to Pole Bank. See pages 13–14 for further details.

Basic route: Minton, Packetstone Hill, Minton Hill, with return by Minton Batch

Minton is a tiny village, a hamlet really, lying back from the A49. Access is by narrow winding lanes from either Marshbrook about a mile to the south-east or from Little Stretton a similar distance to the north-east. A trawl through the library's assembled ranks of history and guide books produced scarcely an enlightening word about Minton save a brief reference to the Domesday Book that suggested it was well and truly at the bottom of the list of revenue raising locations – 'waste it is'. Today's visitor will have a better appreciation of this peaceful spot with its mix of stone, brick and half-timbered houses and a modern-day long house formed by a barn conversion. Birds sing in orchestrated harmony around the tiny village green bright with daffodils in spring and one is reluctant to park a car here. You might like to consider starting this walk from the Long Mynd summit picking it up on The Portway near the Midlands Gliding Club.

From the green take the lane indicated by a 'No Through Road' sign which obscures a bridleway sign. After a few yards turn left up the lane for a short distance to pass through a gateway to enter the National Trust's Minton Hill property.

Make your way uphill by an old quarry with views to your right of Ragleth Hill and, further up the A49, Caer Caradoc. The views improve as quickly as breath is lost. As the fences fall

Small Batch in winter – sheep gather in the valley

122

back continue ahead, climbing steadily with Small Batch to your right.

When the path reaches the point where paths from Small Batch rise to meet it turn left and take the **grassy track** ▶ that rises to Packetstone Hill seen clearly ahead.

The Packet Stone has a wide view to the east with the hills ranging along the A49. To the south-west the forest, looking like the green, hairy head of a giant, comes tumbling down the hillside into Minton Batch. More westerly the bare hills carry the planes of the Midland Gliding Club. Below and heading down towards the forest is the deep declivity of Windy Batch.

From the Packet Stone continue in a north-westerly direction with the path fading a little but still gaining height. The path narrows to follow the edge of the rim above the steep slopes running down to Windy Batch. Above the Batch the path divides. Take the right fork which in about 100 yards will bring you to a small cairn marking the start of a broad track heading north-westerly to meet the road after about a mile. Note the cairn is about 20 yards from the edge of the rim above Windy Batch and care should be taken not to swing too far to the left along the top of the Batch.

The wide track runs across the rolling moorland plateau of Minton Hill still rising a little. The airfield of the Midland Gliding Club comes into closer view. On reaching the road turn left, signed to Plowden and follow the grassy verge for ½ mile to reach the boundary of the gliding club. When the Gliding Club notice is seen ahead take the path signed to Minton Batch on the left. Soon it meets a small stream which will be your companion for the next 2 miles until the road is reached. It doesn't matter which side of the stream you follow at first but eventually you will be obliged to have it on your right-hand side.

Soon you are dipping beneath the hills into a constricted world of grassy slopes, with rushes along the moist edges of the gutter carrying the water off the slopes. Stunted trees dot the hillsides, rocks outcrop here and there. It's a nicely remote and enjoyable descending

This is an old **packhorse route** and the stone gets its name from the local tradition that this is the spot where the animals were rested and their harnesses adjusted. The packhorse was an important way of transporting goods for hundreds of years, a sort of European version of the camel train. Whilst some of the old routes have been swallowed up by modern roads there are many trails over the hills, now used by walkers, along which the lines of pack animals made their way.

THE SHROPSHIRE HILLS – A WALKER'S GUIDE

path. The stream is tiny and it is a surprise to find relatively large fish so close to its source.

The forest edge is reached and the boundary followed on your right, dark ranks of trees, standing shoulder to shoulder with just a glimpse of sun over the top or breaking through to light the narrow passage of a firebreak. The stream coming in from Windy Batch adds its contribution to the waters of Minton Batch and after the forest has retreated a single gorse bush marks the entry to Rams Batch with Shooter's Knoll standing high above.

When the farm is met at the foot of the hill continue forward, crossing a cattle grid, keeping to the broad track with the stream on your right. A small footbridge is crossed to swap the stream to your left. Maintain direction until a junction is made with a lane. Here turn left to reach Minton in about ½ mile. This is a delightful little lane, edged with wild flowers, mouse-ear chickweed, herb robert, violets, buttercups, bluebells, speedwell (surely the walkers emblem, unless that should be the wayfarers tree) yellow archangel, forget-me-not and a late celandine.

Tourist information: Church Street, Church Stretton Tel: 01694 723133 and at National Trust shop Carding Mill Valley

WALK 13

The Three Hills Walk

Maps:	1:25,000 Explorer 217 The Long Mynd & Wenlock Edge; 1:50,000 Landranger 137 Ludlow & Church Stretton
Distance:	5½ miles approx
Car parking:	Easthope Road, Church Stretton (grid ref 453936)
Toilets:	Easthope Road, Church Stretton

Basic route: Church Stretton, Helmeth Hill, Cwms Farm, Willstone Hill, Hope Bowdler Hill, Hope Batch, Hope Bowdler, Church Stretton

The walks in the previous chapters have provided a number of viewpoints from which the hills lining the east side of the A49 have been a very visible part of the landscape, and like the grass on the other side of the track, an incentive for further exploration. This next walk touches upon three of those hills and provides an excellent prospect of the Shropshire countryside.

From the car park turn left along Easthope Road, then right into Sandford Avenue. Just after the post office turn left along Essex Road. After 100 yards or so, as Caer Caradoc comes into view, turn right signposted 'Caradoc and Cardington' to pass behind a residential home. Shortly turn right to cross over the railway tracks; walkers with children should take care to see that they have not run ahead at this point.

Cross over the railway and a field to meet and cross the busy A49. Again take the path signposted to Caradoc and Cardington, through a small, buttercup covered field. Over a stile again, cross a track and continue up a bank into the next field. Follow the path running towards a stile near top right edge of the field to meet a lane.

Here turn left to the top of the lane where there is a beautifully framed view of Caer Caradoc (cameras at the ready if the light is right). Go forward to a point just short of the cattle grid that guards the lane to New House Farm and take the signed footpath that runs half right, following a boundary hedge on your right, beyond which is a deep hollow with a dribble of water. Height is gained gently, the path levelling out to pass between the steep tree-dotted slopes of Caradoc on the left and the more amply covered Helmeth Hill on the right. The path continues as a broad track between fences to pass through a metal gateway. Follow the outside edge of Helmeth Wood, with a pool to your left, where a small group of quietly content mallards have set up home, a very desirable residence for ducks and **woodland birds** ◀.

This is an excellent place for **woodland birds**, and the sharp beaked nuthatch is likely to be seen, a most attractive bird with a black stripe like an extended eyelash running from beak to back of its head. It is a nut and small insect eater and has perfected the technique of descending trees head first. It gets its name from the way it uses the bark of a tree as a wedge to hold a nut whilst using its sharp beak to get at the kernel.

When the path divides to cross a stream ignore the left fork and continue forward for a short distance. Just before the track fords the stream, bear right up a slope to pass through a wicket gate. Continue uphill with the boundary fence of Helmeth Wood to your right. The path rises steadily through bracken and tree covered areas.

Spring walkers may catch the pungent whiff (politely described) of ramson or the more desirable perfume of the bluebells that edge the wood. As height is gained there are good, not to say dramatic, views back to the steep slopes of Caradoc, its full majesty being revealed as this walk progresses.

When the trees fall back the path swings to the left with a wire fence on your right. Soon it passes through a metal gateway, continuing on to a further gateway at the top corner of the field. Once through the gate turn left to follow a path under the bracken covered flank of Hope Bowdler Hill, with its rocky outcrops thrusting up here and there.

The views are improving all the time, the wooded heights of Helmeth, the massive bulk of Caer Caradoc, the gap between them filled with a glimpse of Church Stretton, the tall white posts of the golf course under Haddon Hill and of course the Long Mynd. The ruins of Cwms Farm are passed on your left. Continue forward on the track which is a viewing gallery from which to enjoy the play of light and shadow on Caradoc's vast stage. Caradoc is magnificent, its configuration closely resembling that of a mountain.

Ignore turnings to left and right, maintaining forward direction until a wicket gate is met. Do not pass through, but turn right (roughly south-easterly) on a grassy track running up the hill between Willstone and Hope Bowdler Hills. As the path levels out a stile on the left gives access to Willstone Hill, divert here for a few moments to view the world from the rocky vantage point a little beyond the stile.

To the north-east is the steep and shapely outline of The Wrekin, Church Stretton lies beneath the grey green line of the Long Mynd with The Burway snaking its way above Carding Mill Valley. The Clee Hills are in command to the east, with their giant matchstick men, which others call radio masts, standing guard above Corve Dale; whilst the long wooded ridge of Wenlock Edge runs arrow like above Ape Dale.

Close by the stile, a scatter of wool in a little wire compound testifies to the summer barbering activities that have left the sheep a few pounds lighter and a good deal whiter than they have been for some time. From the

Local farmers, whilst welcoming walkers generally, have stories to tell of thoughtless not to say stupid behaviour in the disturbance to **sheep**. Sheep, considered by some to be low on the intellectual ladder, are sensitive creatures, and represent somebody's livelihood. The wool graders at Bromyard can tell a great deal about a sheep from the condition of its wool and the amount of lanolin present. They can spot a sheep that has been prescribed penicillin or one that has had a fright.

observation point retrace your steps to climb over a stile and turn left to head south on the grassy track which runs across the bracken covered hillside. The curving path presents no difficulty in wayfinding, since there are no obvious alternatives.

As progress is made across the hill between the higher ground of the summits the view to the south opens up presenting an expansive landscape, very different from that explored in the deep hollows and high moorland of the Mynd. The well-wooded heights of the Edge, the green patterned fields of Ape Dale, not great prairies, still retain many trees in their hedgerows. Trees are something you may take for granted but I know people coming to this part of the country from the fenlands for whom the trees make as big an impression as almost anything else. The Clee Hills become more prominent and the smoke that rises in a great column away to your left comes from the Buildwas Power Station, near Ironbridge.

The path swings a little to the west of south, descending on soft springy turf with the symphony of the hills played by a heavenly chorus of larks accompanied by the more earthly bleating of **sheep ◀**.

As the descent above Hope Batch is commenced, **Hope Bowdler** village comes into view, tiny and once much smaller.

Head for the metal gateway and take the broad path which reaches the road by a wooden gate. Here turn

Hope Bowdler

Some family connections in this village go back to the 14th century. The village is tiny, with a few newish, attractively designed houses representing a small expansion from 1975. Once there were just five houses, a school, blacksmith and, of course, the church. Hope Bowdler at the time of the great tax survey, the Domesday Book, was known as Fordritishope and the manor belonged to Edric Sauvage. You may recall that reference was made to him in the Stiperstones walk – Wild Edric, the Saxon man of title that harried the Normans after the conquest. His lands were laid waste and at the time of the survey, 20 years after the conquest, the manor was still listed as such.

128

right into the village, the next turn is to the right opposite the virginia creeper covered Manor Farm but you may like to continue on to the church, St Andrews. From the church retrace your steps back to the Manor Farm entrance and take the path opposite. The wide track curves left and after a short distance turns off along a waymarked path to left of a barn. The path is followed for just over ½ mile to meet the road, where you turn right, soon to pass the entrance to Gaerstones Farm. The stone is prominent on the southern end of Hope Bowdler Hill.

Remain with the road and in 200 yards take the path on the right via a gate and stile and go ahead with a wire fence to your left. At the end of the field, go over a stile and turn right as waymarked, rising with the field edge, ditch and soon Helmeth Hill Wood to the right.

At the top of the field do not turn into the wood but go sharp left to descend towards the cottage, keeping ancient hawthorns and the wire fence to your right. From here there are good views with the white painted, red roofed houses of Church Stretton set, continental style, on the wooded slopes of the Long Mynd whilst the thin line of tarmac that is The Burway climbs steeply to disappear into the bosom of the hills.

Follow the cottage boundary to reach the lane close to the track to New House Farm encountered on the outward journey. On reaching the lane turn left and after a short distance take a path on the right to retrace the outward route back to Church Stretton. One last thought, the crossing of the A49 is a great deal more hazardous than that of the railway line!

Tourist information: Church Street, Church Stretton Tel: 01694 723133 and at National Trust shop Carding Mill Valley

WALK 14

Caractucus's Last Battle

Maps:	1:25,000 Explorer 217 The Long Mynd & Wenlock Edge; 1:50,000 Landranger 137 Ludlow & Church Stretton
Distance:	6 miles approx
Car parking:	Easthope Road, Church Stretton (grid ref 453936)
Toilets:	Easthope Road, Church Stretton (grid ref 453936)

Basic route: Church Stretton, Cardington Old Road, Cwms Cottage, Hill House, Little Caradoc, Caer Caradoc, Church Stretton

Having, as the Victorian novelist would have said, admired Caer Caradoc from afar, this walk will bring about a closer acquaintance. The strange name of the hill reminds us of the son of the ancient British king

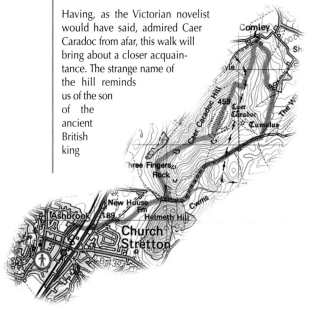

made famous in Shakespeare's Cymbeline. It is worth mentioning that Shropshire has two hill forts of this name, the first is near Clun, but we are concerned with the high and windy ridge that has been in our view at some time during nearly every walk in the hills so far. Spectacular is a word that has been devalued by overuse, but there are few other words that will do.

It is entirely practical to climb this hill from its south-western approach, from the dip between it and Helmeth Hill, but this would be a mistake. It is a great deal more enjoyable to work round the flanks of the hill, ascend from the north-eastern end to make a glorious and long descent over the falling ridge. Caer Caradoc will call the walker back again and again and use of this route will suggest permutations of paths for other expeditions which could include The Wilderness or Caer Caradoc's sister, The Lawley, or an oblique approach via Hope Bowdler Hill.

The start of the walk is the same as the first part of the Hope Bowdler route described in the last walk, up to the edge of Helmeth Wood but a quick resumé here will save leafing back over previous pages.

From the car park in Easthope Road, turn left, then right into Sandford Avenue. After passing the post office turn left to join Essex Road and thereafter take the path signed to the right which passes behind Windsor Place. The railway is crossed, then a field and the A49. Climb over a stile into a short field to cross a lane and enter a further field to exit near the top right edge into another lane. Here turn left along the lane where in June the smell of honeysuckle sweetens the air.

At the top of the lane ignore the first set of footpath signs and go forward for a yard or two to turn right on a footpath just before a cattle grid. (Note: don't set off down the deep hollow way.) The path follows a field boundary on your right, then as it comes to an end, the path is funnelled into a wide track between fences and after a few yards passes through a metal gateway with the slopes of Caer Caradoc to your left and Helmeth Wood rising to the right. Caer Caradoc has its feet in the

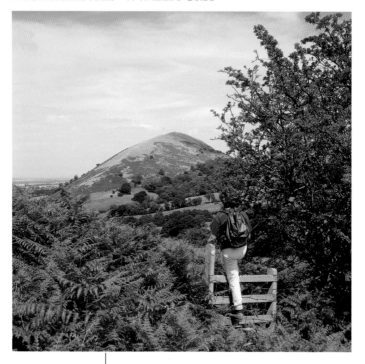

Crossing stile with a view to The Lawley

waters of an attractive little pool – just the place to take the attention of herons.

After about 200 yards take the lesser path that forks off left to cross the stream by a small plank bridge. Once over the stream turn right, for the moment deep in a wooded hollow in the hills. The path soon rises, curving to the left round the lower flanks of Caer Caradoc, soon to meet and turn left on a broader track. The track is the course of an old road to Cardington, popular with walkers and it also still rings to the sound of horses hooves, giving a taste of travel in another age.

The track rises gently, edged with bracken and clumps of rushes where water seeping out of the hillside has kept the ground moist. Caer Caradoc stands proudly

The Lawley

From this position The Lawley resembles, ever so slightly, one of those blanc-mange shapes that trembled on children's party tables.It would take a considerable geological upheaval to cause it to tremble today but we must suppose that just such an event led to its appearance many millions of years ago. The last violent movements along the Church Stretton fault is thought to have occurred at least 200 million years ago and the volcanic rocks that the walker will have noticed outcropping on Caradoc and elsewhere have been dated to over 800 million years. Recent tremors in the Midlands when houses 60 miles or more from the epicentre shook and items fell from cupboards will have dispelled the notion that earthquakes don't happen here anymore.

on the left and to the right the long line of Hope Bowdler Hill, leading on to Willstone Hill. The views are delightful, improving all the time and the ant like figures to be seen on the top of Caer Caradoc are an encouragement to press on to share the pleasures of their hill top adventures.

About ¾ mile from the footbridge a plantation of Scots pine is met. (Note for future reference, a bridleway is signed off here to the right which can be useful in planning walks over Hope Bowdler or Willstone Hill with which it connects). Just beyond the pines, the ruins of Cwms Cottage are passed on the right. The path dips a little and the slopes of The Lawley come into view.

About ¼ mile from the cottage cross a stile on the left to follow a causewayed path running in the direction of the southern end of **The Lawley**.

A short distance along the causewayed path a metal gateway comes into view, head for this and once through continue forward with boundary fence to your right. The long hill to your right is called The Wilderness, although its neatly ordered appearance belies its name. To your left is the shapely Robin's Tump. So shapely that it suggests that nature has been assisted by man, and indeed that may be so since tump is a word used instead of motte ie a flat topped mound carrying a Norman fort.

The path falls to meet and cross a small stream, then a stile to meet a track by Hill House. Here turn left on a signposted path. There is a confusion of several indistinct paths in this area, but after passing a ruined cottage continue forward for about 150 yards to take a path on the right. This follows the edge of a bracken covered field with the boundary to your left, to meet a waymarked stile. Once over the stile, bear half right with The Lawley looking very handsome ahead. Then follow a boundary on your right. At the end of a field pass through a wicket gate and turn left, this time with a hedge to your left. Just short of the next field cross a stile on your left and take the rising footpath that passes under the summit of Little Caradoc.

As height is gained the views improve rapidly. Caer Caradoc itself come into view as the bracken falls away and the clear but steep path to the summit is unveiled. The hill flattens out as a stile is approached, giving a view of the northern end of the Long Mynd with the A49 lying below. Here a reed-edged pool provides water on this dry hillside and damsel flies may be seen, the path to the summit continuing a little beyond this.

It's a stiffish climb to the top but with the comfort of springy turf and, often enough, a cooling breeze to aid progress. A succession of little bumps are met before the summit is reached but the effort is well rewarded and in a few minutes you are passing through the outer bank of the **hill fort** and taking those last few steps equivalent to breaking the tape at the end of a race.

Caer Caradoc Hill Fort

The walker who surveys the landscape from the summit of Caer Caradoc does so from a 6-acre hill fort once the home of the Cornovii. It is a high and windy home, which is enchanting on a summer's day – but what if you were obliged for reasons of security to live up here in the winter? The security is apparent; steeply falling slopes, made more difficult to scale by the engineered banks and ditches, aided by the rocky outcrops used as observation platforms or 'artillery' positions from which stones and arrows could be rained down upon an attacker.

Caer Caradoc with its isolated and pivotal position affords one of the best views in the Shropshire Hills,

Green, green bracken of summer and the drying slopes of The Lawley

allowing the walker to take in the local geography better than anywhere else. As your eye roams the panorama you can trace the routes of past or projected walks as readily as your finger may run over the map. Many opportunities for photography are presented to the walker with the rocky outcrops making a suitable dramatic foreground to set against the distant hills.

In the northern arc The Lawley is the most prominent feature, behind which is seen the wooded slopes of Lodge Hill, from where the eye moves on to the beautifully shaped Wrekin. Below The Lawley lies the little village of Comley. The hills that have edged the A49 for many miles fall back to reveal a field patterning of farmland, broken here and there with small plantations, in winter making the black squares in a somewhat irregular shaped crossword puzzle.

The western view is dominated by the wide expanse of the Long Mynd, its batches and high points seen to perfection and, beyond, there is a glimpse of the higher ridge of the Stiperstones. Beneath the Mynd, road and rail carry their mini cars and little trains, reminiscent of a

Christmas display in the toy department of one of the larger stores. The eastern view takes in the full length of Wenlock Edge overtopped by the ever brooding presence of the Clee Hills. Nearer at hand the Siamese twins of Willstone and Hope Bowdler hills, forever joined together, look smaller now that we view them from above. Southwards, the forested Helmeth Hill is but a stepping stone on to Hazler Hill and then on to the long run of Ragleth Hill. Beyond all this all around in a great and distant bowl, blue grey smudges where sky meets the upthrust land, where other walkers on other hills enjoy their day.

Among the rocky crags of Caer Caradoc

Who was the man who gave this hill its name? Caractacus in the Roman tongue, Caradoc in the English,

Caradawg in the Welsh, carved for himself a place in history and legend.

In the first half of the first century AD Caractacus was the son of a British ruler, Cunobelinus, who for 30 years or so ruled from his capital at Colchester. Fifteen hundred years later Shakespeare made him the subject of his Cymbeline. Following his father's death and the Roman invasion Caractacus, and his brother Togoduninos, led a spirited and heroic campaign against the conquerors. He and his men were badly beaten in a conflict somewhere in the Thames Valley – Wallingford has been suggested as a likely spot – when the Britons fled, seeking safety in the difficult countryside of Essex. The Romans under Aulus Plautius unwisely decided to follow and were in turn obliged to swallow their pride and retire.

The Roman Emperor, Claudius, arrived with reinforcements, including a detachment of elephants, and retrieved the situation with the capture of Colchester, bringing about the end of effective resistance in the southern part of the country. Elusive as ever, Caractacus retreated to Wales and continued his campaign with a series of raids across the border as the Romans endeavoured to extend and consolidate their boundaries.

By AD 47 Ostorios Scapula had succeeded Plautius. By AD 50 he was in a position to put the resistance in the west of the country under pressure and in that year the final battle took place. Where? The British Camp in the Malvern Hills has been claimed as the site of Caractacus's defeat, but our hill fort named after this ancient hero seems just as likely. On the outskirts of Church Stretton an area known and shown on the map as Battle Field is locally believed to be the site of the final clash. If so, was Caractacus caught unawares and away from his hilltop stronghold, or did the battle range over a wider area with an assault on the fort part of the conflict?

Wheresoever it was that the battle took place, the result was decisive. Caractacus's wife, daughters and other relatives were taken prisoner. Caractacus again escaped and according to legend hid in a cave beneath the western side of Caer Caradoc. Defeated, he travelled north to the land of the Brigantes, but their Queen, perhaps sensing the way the wind was blowing, handed him over to the Romans.

Caractacus and his family were sent to Rome, to be put on show at a victory parade. Britain was to the ordinary Roman citizen a mysterious land and crowds gathered for the event. To their surprise paraded before them was not a defeated downcast figure, but a man of dignity with head held high, who had fought a good fight and had lost and in losing had earned the respect of the victors.

Caractacus was a considerable fighter but it is clear he must have been a consummate politician as well in keeping the resistance going over the years of the invasion. It was this skill he used to persuade the Emperor Claudius to spare his life and that of his family. Caractacus died within a few short years but legend has it that his children were converted to Christianity and in the course of time returned to Britain bringing the faith to their native land.

From the fort head south-west along the falling summit ridge towards Three Finger Rock; the reason for its name becoming quickly apparent. Beyond the rock a track runs forward towards Helmeth Wood, quickly falling off the hill to meet a broad track at the foot. Here turn right and after a short distance, left over the little plank bridge to turn right and retrace the steps of your outward journey back to Church Stretton.

Tourist information: Church Street, Church Stretton Tel: 01694 723133 and at National Trust shop Carding Mill Valley

Other places of interest are as listed in Walk 10 but with a reminder that if you are holidaying in the area, Shrewsbury, although outside the scope of this book, should not be forgotten.

WALK 15

An Englishman's Home

Maps:	1:25,000 Explorer 217 The Long Mynd & Wenlock Edge and Explorer 203 Ludlow; 1:50,000 Landranger 137 Ludlow & Church Stretton
Distance:	5½ miles approx
Car parking:	Lay-by on A49, Stokesay (grid ref 437819). There is also a car park for visitors to the castle further up the Stokesay lane
Toilets:	Nearest are at Craven Arms, unless visiting the castle

Basic route: Stokesay, Stoke Wood, Clapping Wicket, View Wood, View Edge, Gorst Barn, Aldon, Stoke Wood, Stokesay

This walk is ideal for those combining it with a visit to **Stokesay Castle**, providing a flavour of past life in this border area with quite excellent views of the countryside in which it is set.

The midland counties of England bore much of the turmoil of the Civil War, and Stokesay was not excused from duty. In the early days of the conflict it served as a supply base for the King at nearby Ludlow. Stokesay came under attack by superior forces

Stokesay Castle

Stokesay Castle is a fine example of a fortified manor house; a handsome group of buildings of considerable interest and antiquity, deservedly much photographed, and a great pleasure to visit. It might very well have been lost, for such places are expensive to maintain and require much loving and knowledgeable care in their preservation. In the 19th century the castle was falling into dereliction but happily it was rescued and resuscitated by the Worcester glover, John Allcroft. Today Stokesay is in the care of English Heritage. At the time of the Norman conquest Edric Sylvaticus held Stokesay and it was occupied by Aeldred. Edric declared his allegiance to William but, having thought better of his oath, forfeited the estate.

In the reign of Henry I (1115) the North Tower was built during the occupancy of the de Say family. One hundred and fifty years later great fortunes were being made in the wool trade, and a Ludlow merchant, Lawrence, bought the estate which passed on to successive generations of his family. In the Elizabethan era it came into the ownership and occupancy of Sir George and Sir Arthur Mainwaring, during which time the splendid gatehouse was built. The Craven family owned Stokesay from the days of Charles I through to the mid 19th century.

Stokesay Castle – the North Tower

and discretion being the better part of valour, was surrendered. It was again the centre of military action in April 1645 when it was the turn of the Royalists under Sir William Croft to assail the castle. A brave but abortive attack left many dead including Sir William. As a result of its use as a base in support of the King, the outer curtain wall was reduced in size, the 'slighting' mild in comparison with many other places which were left little better than ruins.

Stokesay Castle – this is just the gatehouse!

From the lay-by off the A49 (on the Stokesay side of the road) walk southwards for a short distance and take the lane on the right signed to Stokesay Castle. The lane passes the church entrance – if visiting the church turn left through the lych gate with its **mounting block** ▶, a relic of the days when the better-off came to church by horse.

The castle gatehouse seen framed by the lych gate is a popular photographic shot. The church is also well worth a visit.

Keep with the lane as it edges past the castle grounds. Ignore the first footpath off to the right and continue past a pool to take a signed path on the right. After passing barns on your left go forward and cross a railway line and continue forward on a broad track to reach a metal gate. Enter a field and cross to a stile seen almost opposite, then continue forward to a further stile. Once over this cross a further field to a stile at the edge of a wood. This last stile is hidden from sight until you reach it. A backward glance as progress is made will provide good views of Stokesay and the rolling countryside, but the best is yet to come.

Mounting blocks
are often to be found outside inns and churches. I have wondered what people did with their horses whilst at their Sunday devotions. Were they tethered to the church gate, or left to graze the churchyard thus alleviating the vicar's age old problem of trying to keep the grass down?

141

A few paces into the wood turn right along a bracken and conifer edged path which is followed for just under ½ mile to reach Clapping Wicket. Emerge from the wood by large ash trees and an old house. On leaving the wood go forward a few paces then turn left uphill towards (but not to enter) the wood. On reaching the fence bear right, following the outside edge of the wood with excellent views to the west. At the end of the field cross a stile and continue almost to the end of the next field to join a broad track on the left. Follow it through the wood. Emerge into the open after about 200 yards. Here bear left up the hillside with the wood on your left. Close to the top of the rise join a narrow waymarked path which enters the wood to meet a clearer path. Turn right, climbing through a hollow way to reach a way-marked stile. Once over the stile continue forward on what in summer is an overgrown path to meet the road by View Edge Farm with its well tended gardens.

The westward views are splendid and these will soon be complemented by the eastward prospect. Turn left along the lane and in a short distance take a path on the right over a stile, soon to see the familiar shapes of Brown Clee and Titterstone Clee Hills. Follow the outside edge of a wood to the end of the field and cross a stile to enter a further field. Gaps in the trees give further excellent views to the west: a succession of wooded heights which includes Sunny Hill – the site of Bury Ditches, an Iron Age fort. Continue forward with the wooded area falling steeply away, to a stile, a little to the left of the bottom corner of a field.

Once over the stile continue on with a hedge on your left. Almost at the end of the field, turn left through an old gateway into a further field which may be under crops. If the path is indistinct, remember that it runs roughly in line with the lone tree on the opposite hill. At the bottom of the field pass through a double gateway and bear diagonally left up the rise to follow a broad track, soon to pass Gorst Barn on your left. Pass through a metal gateway and pursue the track for about 200 yards to meet a lane.

Turn left and follow the quiet country lane, edged with coppiced hazel and honeysuckle in season, to reach Aldon in just under a mile. At the top of a hill a sometimes dried-up pond signals the edge of Aldon, a small farming settlement with stone barns and houses and excellent views to Titterstone Clee Hill.

The lane curves through the hamlet. On meeting a T-junction turn left and, in about 200 yards, take a track on the right, joining a high level route that gives good views. Over a gate Ludlow can be seen in the distance with its church tower rather easier to find than the castle.

The track enters woodland, in July providing a splash of colour as rosebay willowherb comes into bloom – not for nothing is it called fireweed. Continue through the wood with a glimpse of the River Onny snaking through the valley towards Onibury. On leaving the wood pass over a crossing track and a waymarked stile to descend to the bottom left edge of the field. Here climb over a stile and go forward on a broad track to meet and cross the railway, turning left on a metalled lane to return past Stokesay Castle to your starting point.

Tourist information: Castle Street, Ludlow Tel: 01584 875053

Stokesay Castle (English Heritage): Craven Arms. Open May–Aug daily. Mar–Apr, Sept–Oct: Wed–Sun. Nov–Feb: Thurs–Sun.

Shropshire Hills Discovery Centre: The Centre is found at Craven Arms – impressive modern architecture, a single-storey building in the round and topped by a turf roof. Onny Meadows Nature Study, an exciting exhibition, café and events. Open daily. Summer 10am–5.30pm. Winter 10am–4.30pm.

Stella Mitchell's Land of Lost Content – a National Museum of British Popular Culture: The Market Hall, Market Street, Craven Arms. Open 11–5 daily, closed Dec. Tel: 01588 676176

FEATURE 4

Ludlow

Ludlow is surely one of the finest small towns in the country, with great architectural riches. Let me quote one impressive statistic – the town has no fewer than 469 listed buildings, proof of the pleasures that are waiting to be enjoyed by visitors with time to make a leisurely tour of this hilltop town. The exploration is aided by the use of the excellent Ludlow Walks leaflet produced by the Civic Society which has also been responsible for fixing blue plaques to a number of buildings of special interest.

The quality of Ludlow's buildings reflects the town's prosperity, which was aided by geographical, political and economic factors. Ludlow's long development began following the Norman invasion of England when the new masters of the country built a series of castles as part of the strategy to secure their western borders against the Welsh. The building of the castle triggered the growth of the town. The security of living beneath the castle walls must have had a considerable appeal. The strategic importance of Ludlow also made it a focal point for trade and the town developed as a market and a prosperous centre of the woollen industry. Today's Castle Square is part of the 12th-century market place which extended from the castle to the Bullring.

The town's further prosperity was ensured by the castle's establishment as the seat of the Council of the Marches. This administrative body grew in power and in the reign of Henry VIII had its permanent quarters in the castle from which it continued to rule Wales and the border counties of Shropshire, Herefordshire, Worcestershire and Gloucestershire until it was abolished in 1689. This 'regional seat of government' made Ludlow an even busier place and some of Ludlow's well known buildings date from this time when fine houses were built for those engaged in the business of the council. Later, Ludlow, like Worcester, was an important centre of the glove industry.

Ludlow is set high above the River Teme with its streets rising to the centre of the town with its castle, market place and church. The 'classic' view of Ludlow which is so often seen in the guides to Britain is that from Whitcliffe – a handsome prospect, which is seen to best advantage when the sun has moved into the west to fully light the scene. Above the trees rise the walls of the castle and the tall tower of the fine parish church with the Clee Hills providing a backdrop that confirms this as one of the finest views of a town and its countryside. It is at its most dramatic not on a day of clear blue skies but when clouds driven by a strong wind produce alternating periods of shade and light. Sometimes with just the castle or church tower lit, or the town standing blackly against the brightness of the distant hills, a scene that may soon, like a photographic negative be reversed.

Then there is the river, best enjoyed from the 15th-century Ludford Bridge. Here the fast flowing waters, released from the restraints of the weir, come tumbling down over a rocky course, a pleasure that may be enhanced by a bright flash of colour as a kingfisher darts upstream to another perch. The youth hostel is in Ludford Lodge, delightfully situated by the bridge.

There is another fine view of the river from the topmost tower of the Castle, here above the weir this is Shropshire's counterpart to the view of the Avon from Warwick Castle, with swallows skimming low over the water, the splash of oars from little boats and the paddles of brightly coloured canoes. It is also in a measure reminiscent of Richmond, that splendid Yorkshire stronghold with the Swale running beneath the castle walls.

The strength of the castle is apparent even in its partial roofless state, with its strategic position on the Marches commanding the river, the north–south road and the approaches from the west. A special feature of interest is the round tower of the chapel of St Mary Magdalene, one of only a handful of circular churches in the country.

Castles are by their very nature exciting places, an irresistible magnet quickly bringing all sorts of images to

Castle from Dinham

the mind. Ludlow is very satisfactory in this respect, with its curtain wall, high ramparts and keep, with little dark passages linking the great halls and winding stone stairways.

Royalty would have been entertained here, perhaps their favours sought, or maybe the boot was on the other foot and the King was here to seek to assure himself of the undying loyalty of the lord who held the castle. In the Great Chamber the eyes of past monarchs gaze stonily down upon us and maybe the cold stones will encourage a little shiver when we read that it was the all powerful owner Roger Mortimer who was responsible for the horrific murder of Edward II at Berkeley Castle in 1327. Three years later the hand of retribution struck and Mortimer was hung, drawn and quartered at Tyburn.

The Castle is associated with another contentious chapter in the history of the monarchy. The 'Princes in the Tower', the alleged illegitimate Edward V together with his younger brother, lived here, Edward as Prince of Wales until his accession to the throne in 1483 at the age of 12. Their removal to the Tower of London, and subsequent murder, has engaged both historians and writers of historical dramas over a long period.

The man who might have been King was also resident in Ludlow. He was Prince Arthur, heir to Henry VII and whilst still an infant betrothed to Catherine of Aragon. The marriage took place when he was 15 but within a few months Arthur, never a strong boy, died. His fine chantry tomb is to be seen in Worcester Cathedral. So it was that when Henry VII died in 1509 it was a larger than life man that succeeded to the throne – the one King that everybody knows at least something about even if it is only as a serial bridegroom. The rest is history.

Of all the buildings in the town the one that is the most photographed is surely the handsome half-timbered Feathers Hotel, once the home of Rees Jones, a Pembrokeshire man who came to the town as an attorney at the Council of the Marches. His initials are to be found on the lock plate and the fine carvings on the door lintels demand attention. His home became an inn in 1670, with later alterations including the addition of a balcony for electioneering.

Timber framed building decoration at its finest – Ludlow's Feathers Hotel

The Feathers, which has been described as a treasure house, inside and out, is not the town's oldest inn. That honour falls to The Bull Inn. Approached from the little alley from the churchyard it presents the familiar film set image of an inn, with a wide entrance through which coaches would bring their passengers. Amongst the town's many handsome buildings must be numbered the double jettied premises at the corner of Broad Street.

The town has a network of alleys, short cuts well used by the residents, which the visitor gradually discovers. You may return again and again to Ludlow and each time see something different, elaborate little carvings on buildings previously missed. Places like the Reader's House, a tall three-storied wood framed building behind the church, with leaded lights, an iron studded door and carved arch above the window grill.

The Reader's House, Ludlow

The most prominent building on the skyline is the cathedral-like church which has attracted the attention of many famous writers of the past. The church guide is the most detailed I have seen of any parish church but then there is much to be appreciated. Not the least the monuments which reflect the period of the Council of the Marches. There is the colourful monument erected by Edward Waties to commemorate himself and his wife Martha who died in 1629. This favoured position in the chancel reflects his membership of the Council of the Marches and his marriage.

There is a fine tomb to Edmund Walter and his wife Mary. Edmund Walter was Chief Justice of the Shires in South Wales and a member of His Majesty's Council for the Marches of Wales. Rivalling this is the tomb of Sir Robert Townshend and his wife Alice. He too was a Justice of the Council of the Marches.

The church is dedicated to St Laurence and the east window depicts a series of events in the life of the saint including his repeated beatings and torture and martyrdom on the gridiron. The choir stalls are of great interest with elaborate carvings and numerous misericords which depict a wide variety of seemingly bizarre subjects. These include a fox disguised as a bishop preaching to a flock of geese; a mermaid with the traditional comb and mirror; a woman with extravagant horned head wear; and retribution falling upon an alewife notorious for giving short measure – all very popular subjects for the photographer.

Adjoining the church are the Hosyer's Almshouses, a handsome town-hall like building originally built in 1486 and restored and extended in 1758. Other buildings which will take the interest are the Buttercross, rebuilt in 1743 and which once housed the Bluecoat Charity School, and the Tolsey. A plaque on the wall records 'The Tolsey, 15th century acts and charters of Edward IV and VI governed the taking of tolls on market goods, Court of Pied Powder, (or dusty feet) for the summary justice of market offences such as dishonest trading and restrictive practices. Extensively repaired in 1624 when 2500 pinnes were needed. Saved from demolition and restored 1963–64 by the efforts of the owner, Mrs Hardy, the Ludlow Town Council, Shropshire County Council, Historic Buildings Trust and the Ludlow Society'. It now does duty as a fruit and vegetable shop.

Most towns have their museums and Ludlow is no exception with an array of exhibits telling something of its history from the Norman Conquest. Under the heading of crime and punishment we are introduced to some barbaric items: a torture mask of about 1630 which was discovered hidden in the castle wall. The gradual tightening of screws was intended to extract information from prisoners with a branding iron used to leave permanent scarring on the face. We are informed that the Court of the Marches was expected to torture 'when they should think convenient those suspected of treason, murder or felonies'. A man trap dating from 1710 used to deter poachers and the like, hardly seems less kindly and only became illegal in the middle of the 19th century. (A strong inducement to walkers of the day to keep to the footpath.)

One man's punishment was another man's living and the museum quotes from accounts, for example in 1565 a rope to bind prisoners and to hang a man was charged at sixpence. In 1569 a charge of 24 pence is recorded for whipping vagabonds whilst a few years later a Richard Hall is given 24 pence for nailing three men to the pillory. In the next century a man that carried a ladder to and from the execution site was rewarded with fourpence.

A whole variety of items build a picture of life in the town – a Victorian sitting room with a lady in the dress of 1885. Old photographs showing the fire brigade with its hand drawn pumps and the laying of the first electricity cable in 1906. The sensation of 1913 was an aeroplane display. In 1817 a Signor Riviletto visited the town with what can best be described as a one man band. His performance was advertised to end with Rule Britannia and God Save the King upon eight instruments at one time! Walkers giving their boots a day off will find much of absorbing interest in Ludlow.

Tourist information: Castle Street, Ludlow Tel: 01584 875053
St Laurence's Church: Open daily
Ludlow Castle: Open daily except Christmas Day, Sat–Sun only Jan
Ludlow Museum: 10.30–1, 2–5 Mon–Sat Easter–end Oct, also Sun Jun–Aug

WALK 16

Forest Walking at High Vinnals

Maps:	1:25,000 Explorer 203 Ludlow; 1:50,000 Landranger 137 Ludlow & Church Stretton
Distance:	6 miles approx
Car parking:	Forest Enterprise car park about 3 miles south-west of Ludlow on Wigmore Road (grid ref 474731)
Toilets:	None on site

Basic route: Vinnals car park, High Vinnals, Climbing Jack Common, Mary Knoll Valley

Following the First World War the government established the Forestry Commission in an effort to ensure an improving home supply of timber, reserves of which had been further depleted by the desperate needs of a war economy. Today the Commission cares for millions of acres of forest throughout the country and it is to them that landowners turn for expert advice.

New forests are being created with 12 large amenity forests being established close to urban areas. The Forestry Commission will be actively involved in this work, it has the hallmark of a useful and exciting long-term project. In the Midlands the regeneration of some of the old mining areas is being assisted by the National Forest. Whilst many will think of the Forestry Commission as supplying the demands for softwood from its coniferous forests it is engaged in the production of other, longer maturing trees, as the oak plantations seen during the course of the walk will demonstrate.

The Commission through it's Forest Enterprise arm is generous in allowing access to its forests, welcoming in the provision of car parks, picnic sites, waymarked trails and educational facilities, which extend beyond the needs

Note: This walk has been revised since the first edition of this book was published to take into account various changes within the forest. It should be noted that from time to time Forest Enterprise's waymarked walks may be subject to change so that references to the coloured waymarker posts which had been used as an aid to describing this route have been excluded with the exception of the Mortimer Trail, which is followed for about 2¼ miles in the middle section of the walk.

of good public relations. The information board at Vinnals car park shows three colour coded waymarked walks. Elsewhere further routes may be found at Bury Ditches and Croft Ambrey, which visit hill forts.

A feature of the forest is the herd of long coated fallow **deer** ◄ of a kind found nowhere else in the world.

The walk which follows combines elements of various waymarked routes taking the walker up to a high viewpoint, along broad rides or by narrow paths into the depths of the forest, a pleasing combination which should dispel any misgivings you may have about the monotony of some forest walking.

There are some 500 **deer** in the forest but seeing them does require a quiet passage along the paths and an element of luck. Watching for their tracks (slots) on softer ground may at least give the satisfaction of confirming their presence.

The walk starts from the Forest Enterprise's Vinnals car park to head south. Take the broad forest track on the western side of the car park, initially with an open field to your right. About 400 yards from the road a small pond and picnic site is seen below to your right. Continue with the winding, rising and falling forest road with the thickly tree covered slopes of High Vinnals to your left. Ignore any minor turnings.

About a mile from your starting point a strong curve left is made, still with the main track. A pond on your left will confirm you are on the correct route as will a deep ditched stream. About 350 yards from the pond, bend left soon crossing the culverted stream. The climbing way takes a serpentine course and after heading south meets a junction where it curves left with the forest road, now northwards, to make a junction with a further road in 400 yards.

Turn right and in a further 400 yards left. In a little over 100 yards turn left again on the waymarked Mortimer Trail. The wide track climbs with improving views to reach an observation tower in ½ mile. Here the view westward is a wide mosaic of forest and field with half a hundred grey smudged hills rolling away to the Welsh Marches. Looking back to the south on a clear day the Black Mountains near Abergavenny may be recognised by those familiar with that territory.

Continue northwards, with good views, to a turning circle, go forward on a narrow and more steeply falling path. After about 100 yards the path divides, keep with the right curve, still on the Mortimer Trail. Ignore turns both left and right, descending to emerge into the open grass and bracken of Climbing Jack Common in about ¼ mile. Now there are good views to the east with Brown Clee Hill and Titterstone Clee Hill identified by the white globe of the satellite station. Southwards, Worcestershire's Abberley and Woodberry Hills, with the Clock Tower, which is the county's answer to Big Ben, between the two may be seen.

Continue over the common and into woodland again, your direction being just a little south of east, to meet a forest road (about ¾ mile from the point where you first met the common). Cross the road to maintain your way along the Mortimer Trail also marked as a permissive path, a falling path with a deep ditch to the left. In 400 yards a four way junction is met. Turn left with coniferous trees on the left and broad leaf on the right. The path descends towards the Mary Knoll Valley with, in winter at least, the almost ghostly white image of Sunny Dingle Cottage seen through the trees and the ceaseless chatter of a distant stream.

On meeting a forest road in the valley bottom turn left with it. In a few yards leave the Mortimer Trail to go its own way to Ludlow as it crosses the stream. Remain with the forest road, with the stream at varying distances to your right, for 1½ miles to a T-Junction and take the right-hand signed track to return to the car park.

Tourist information: Castle Street, Ludlow Tel: 01584 875053

WALK 17
Offa's Dyke

Maps:	1:25,000 Explorer 201 Knighton & Presteigne; 1:50,000 Landranger 137 Ludlow & Church Stretton
Distance:	7 miles approx
Car parking:	Crabtree Lane off West Street, Knighton (grid ref 285726). Small car park Crabtree Lane and main long-stay car park, Bowling Green Lane by cattle market.

Basic route: Knighton, Teme Bank, Panpunton Hill, Cwm-sanaham Hill, Brynorgan, eastern flank Cwm-sanaham and return as outward

If Offa had not built his Dyke, and more importantly if his name had not become irremovably attached to it, then it is doubtful if he would be known to many people. The renewed controversy over who and when the Dyke was built is unlikely to upset Offa's place in history for this was indeed his established western frontier in name and fact.

Offa came to the throne of Mercia in AD 757 and during the course of a reign which spanned 40 years, achieved recognition beyond the strict bounds of his territory, creating what we would today call a sphere of influence, and becoming generally known as the King of the English.

The length of his reign must surely confirm Offa as an astute ruler with both military and political skills. In those distant days it is scarcely likely that he would have survived so long without both those attributes in generous measure. He came to power at a time of upheaval. His almost immediate predecessor, Aethelbald, had enjoyed a long and largely peaceful reign, from AD 716, but towards the end of that time his hold upon the country from the

Humber southwards was considerably weakened. Three years before Aethelbald's violent death, murdered apparently by those entrusted with his protection, he had sustained a substantial defeat at Burford. As a result, Wessex operated under its own rule, the Welsh were becoming increasingly difficult and the East Angles, East Saxons and the Kentish men no longer bowed the knee. A shrinking and vulnerable kingdom, which was a prize for the taking or easy pickings for raiders was how it might have appeared to those with covetous eyes.

'Uneasy lies the head that wears a crown' is Shakespeare's oft quoted line from Henry IV, but it could equally well have been written for Offa coming to the throne in a period of violent unrest that followed Aethelbald's death. Clearly there was a need to put his house in order, strengthen his kingship and make it safe from attack from within and without. He seems to have spent 14 careful, patient years doing just that.

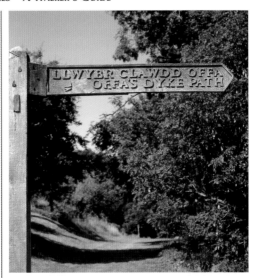

Offa's Dyke Path signing – Welsh and English

Not until Offa's home base was strong and secure did he set out to recoup lost territory, pushing out the borders of Mercia once again. AD 771 marked the conquest of the Hestingi (of Sussex), four years later the Kentish forces were defeated at Otford and henceforth bent the knee. The East Saxons gave way to him and London was his. He turned his attentions to the West Saxons and defeated their king, Cynewulf, at Benson on the Thames. This victory opened up the way to the recovery of land lost by Aethelbald following his defeat at the Battle of Burford in AD 754. Oxford and the land to its north came under Offa's control together with the high downland rising above the Thames from Goring, territory well known, and loved, by walkers heading west along the Ridgeway Path.

The Welsh were next to be obliged to retreat, and Offa secured the land beyond the River Severn, freeing it from the incursions to which it had been subject. He drew a line upon the ground making a clear statement that beyond this they should not pass. This was Offa's

Dyke, a political and defensive frontier earthwork that stretched from the Dee in the North to the Wye's junction with the Severn in the South. This determination to impose the rule of law brought peace and harmony to the borders – but not for ever.

If all this sounds like a warrior king, then we must redress the balance with a brief reference to his other accomplishments. Offa's activities brought stability, Pope Hadrian is known to have acknowledged him as the King of the English. He is said to have been a religious man, generous to the monastic institutions. He arranged a yearly payment to assist the poor of Rome and to provide lighting in St Peters. In this connection some writers suggest that in effect he established the precedent for 'Peter's Pence' a tax that was levied for over 600 years until Henry VIII brought about the split with Rome.

A country is often judged by the strength of its currency (then as today). Offa was responsible for the minting of the silver penny, which of course bore the King's head to vouch for its authenticity. They came into wide usage – an undoubted mark of confidence in the stability of the established government.

The building of the Dyke was a considerable enterprise; that it was carried to a satisfactory conclusion and apparently achieved the desired effect can only reinforce the impression that Offa was a man of great resolve, strength and ability.

That he seems to have died peacefully was in itself the greatest tribute to his restoration of order to a troubled kingdom. He is said to have been buried in a chapel near Bedford but there is no shrine to which those minded to do so can make a pilgrimage. In remembering that it was defensive, that it brought a measure of peace and stability (for a time at least) to the borderland, we may like to think of his Dyke as a more fitting memorial.

In this book we can only sample a short stretch of **Offa's Dyke Path** as it passes through the rather arbitrary boundaries chosen to illustrate the walking pleasures available in this area of the Midlands. Those who having tasted of the fruit and feel moved to pursue it further may

Offa's Dyke Path

Offa's Dyke was a natural choice for a long distance footpath, National Trail as they are now called. In its 168-mile journey along the border country, it passes through two Areas of Outstanding Natural Beauty and touches upon the Brecon Beacons National Park. There is a variety of scenic contrast from river valleys to high moorland. It should not be thought that the path follows the Dyke throughout, (indeed there is only about 80 miles of the Dyke visible) but the spirit of the path is always present. Those who know the deep ditch and bank of the Wansdyke in Wiltshire, for example, may be a little disappointed in the Dyke itself. The Dyke as seen today is never quite as dramatic as might be expected and can in many places be only described as modest. So much so that on a recent walk in the Knighton area I fell into conversation with two walkers and asked where they were heading and was told that they were looking for the Dyke – I was obliged to tell them that they had been walking on it for the last mile! Never fear it's not always quite so invisible.

find my guide *Walking Offa's Dyke Path* helpful. It provides a detailed walking and historical guide to the full route and is published by Cicerone. Long distance walking apart there are sections of the trail that are ideal for round walks, the Wye Valley between Monmouth and Chepstow – the Dyke is on the English side of the river – the Black Mountains and the Clywydian Hills.

This walk starts from the car park at the foot of Crabtree Lane, Knighton (off West Street) close to the River Teme, but a visit to the Heritage Centre close by in West Street may be of interest. The park has stones commemorating the opening of 'Llwybr Clawdd Offa, Offa's Dyke Path, from Prestatyn to Sedbury Cliffs, 168 miles opened here July 10 1971 by Lord Hunt, CBE DSO' and a further stone erected by the Offa's Dyke Association which is inscribed 'Clawdd Offa, Offa's Dyke, King of Mercia AD 757–796 marks the 80 miles of the boundary of Wales, the most impressive work of the old English King.'

At the outset it should be suggested that the best of the walk might have its greatest appeal by simply following the acorn waymarked route for as long as you feel inclined and then retracing your steps back to Knighton.

Nevertheless, an alternative is offered here; even so it involves retracing a good stretch of your outward route.

From the car park head upstream along the riverside path soon passing a Welcome to Wales sign – which we are in fact just leaving! The path follows the river, via a series of kissing gates, for about ¼ mile. In summer it is a delight to watch the river activity, swifts swoop and dive in an amazing display of high speed aerobatics as they feed off the insects.

Cross the river by a footbridge then, immediately, the railway track to a stile, at first almost hidden by the bridge wall. In 50 yards the path bears right and crosses a further stile seen a short distance ahead. After crossing a lane pass through a metal gateway. From here a long steep climb begins, your payment for the pleasure of the views which are to come. Follow a broad rising track with the wood edge to your right. This steep track lifts the walker high above the Teme valley with views to the shapely hills that fill the landscape, a mix of woodland, bracken and pasture.

At the top of the slope, by a wire fence, turn sharp left as directed by the finger post to pursue a generally north-west direction, soon to pass a conifer plantation on your right and following the line of the Dyke. After the plantation the path narrows with fence to the right. Knighton is seen in its setting beneath the hills.

The river takes a meandering leisurely course down the valley, whilst the railway makes a more purposeful progress on its scenic way through Wales. There is level walking for a spell, then cross over a stile beyond which there is a memorial which reads 'Roy Waters, Tref-y-Clawdd 1970 Society. We remember Roy Waters, chairman of the Society from 1970–1980'. Continue onwards, here the path is hemmed in a little by barbed wire on the fence to your right and nature's own barbed wire on the left, gorse bushes, which scratch the legs of the unwary.

When a broad crossing track is met (running east–west) bear right with it for a few yards, then left again to follow the Dyke, which here in this sloping field looks like a sleeping giant. Another fir plantation is met and a stile crossed to restore the fencing to your right once more. Continue on the outside of the plantation with the path falling and rising switchback fashion with the triangulation point on Cwm-sanaham Hill signalling the next high point.

As the path recovers some height from its last swoop down, a further broad crossing track is met with bridle-ways signed left and right. From this small crossroads of the hills take the steep narrow path, stepped here and there, which winds up to the summit of Cwm-sanaham Hill (1328 feet). This is a good place to stop for refreshment and to take in the view with the triangulation point making a convenient back rest. Just 3 miles further on the Dyke reaches its maximum height, an extra 80 feet, on Llanfair Hill, where it also improves its image with a more impressive section.

From the triangulation point cross a stile to follow the Dyke, pock-marked here and there by holes; ankle turning traps for the unwary. As the fence falls back the path swings half right and downhill to stile seen ahead.

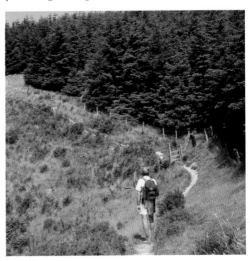

*Offa's Dyke Path near
Cwm-sanaham Hill*

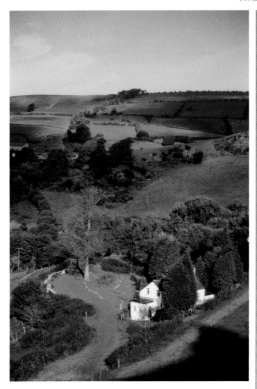

Offa's Dyke Path looking north to the house at Brynorgan with the dyke climbing towards Llanfair Hill

Once over the stile the narrow, single tread path drops steeply down the hillside, as directed by marker posts. From here the path is seen clear ahead as it makes its run up to the summit of Llanfair Hill. Closer at hand, down in the dip is the white house of Brynorgan.

Head down towards the house, which is reached after crossing a small trickle of a stream. If you have elected to take the partly circular walk rather than a there and back excursion, take the right-hand track by Brynorgan with its rhyming instructions 'Be ye men or be ye woman, Be ye early or be ye late, be ye coming or be ye going, Please don't forget to shut the gate'.

Follow the wide track from Brynorgan which runs between hedges of coppiced hazel, elderberry and holly – a nicely shaded lane further decorated with digitalis and dog rose. A metal gate is reached as the path begins to descend just short of the road. Once through the gateway, turn right on a broad rising track. Bwlch Farm is seen in the valley below, the narrow winding lanes disappearing into the distance. Bwlch is just two houses, a couple of sheds – and a barn that appears to occupy a bigger area than the rest put together. The eye is sent roaming over the well ordered rolling landscape, forest, pasture, with hills dressed in green and brown. An old quarry is passed, from which the stone may have been taken to surface this track or build the scatter of houses.

Continue forward with the boundary fence to your left. After a while the stony track changes to a softer tread. Continue towards the long line of trees seen ahead, perhaps planted as a windbreak. As the trees sweep away to the east, leave them to go their own way and continue forward rising over the crest of the hill. Just before a farm building is reached, bear right, passing conifer plantation to rejoin Offa's Dyke path under the southern end of Cwm-sanaham Hill. Here turn left to retrace your steps back to Knighton.

Tourist information: Offa's Dyke Heritage Centre, West Street, Knighton Tel: 01547 528753.

WALK 18

More on Offa

Maps:	1:25,000 Explorer 201 Knighton & Presteigne; 1:50,000 Landranger Sheet 137 Ludlow & Church Stretton
Distance:	6½ miles approx (or Offa's Dyke only 3 miles)
Car parking:	No formal car parking
Toilets:	Nearest in Knighton

Basic route: Selley Hall, Garbett Hall, Llanfair Hill, Bwlch, Llanfair Waterdine, Graig, Selley Cross

This round walk follows the dyke to its highest point on Llanfair Hill and after descending to Bwlch makes a return by country lanes and old roads. Whilst by no means without their interest you may agree with me that the walking may be enjoyed in fullest measure by sticking to the Dyke. If walking from Knighton to the triangulation point on Llanfair Hill and back, the distance is about 10 miles. If the Dyke is joined from the road to the north of Brynorgan, then the trip to the summit and back measures just under 3 miles.

The walk starts a little to the north of Brynorgan and is reached from Knighton by taking the road towards the station then turning left to follow under Panpunton Hill and forking right at Skyborry Green on the Clun Road.

There is space to leave two or three cars on the verge just beyond the spot where Offa's Dyke Path crosses the road near Selley Hall. The signed path rises from the road to cross a stile, then climbs towards a clump of larch trees, with the Dyke to your right. A short steep scramble soon provides good views. Walk forward along the top of

the
Dyke and,
after a short distance, lose
height, again by the Dyke,
which at this point has widened.
Cross a broad intersecting track and go forward to a
little plank bridge built by the Royal Engineers in 1985. A
further bridge is crossed, shortly to be followed by a stile
to meet the road by Garbett Hall. Cross the road and
pass through a metal gate to bear right past farm buildings. The way ahead is now clear, a broad, steadily rising
track which follows the course of the dyke.

Small gorse bushes add a touch of yellow either side
of the track in season and the quality of the Dyke is
improving: deeper and higher. Larch trees line the bank
and the trek up to the summit affords a splendid prospect
of the rolling border country.

Walkers on the Dyke, Llanfair Hill

The way levels out for a while and crosses a track, soon to follow the Dyke to the summit triangulation point, which is tucked up against a fence, a little to the western side of the Dyke. The spot height here is 430 metres, but more grandly measured in feet at 1410.

This is a natural turning point for those making a there-and-back exploration of the **Dyke ▶**. Here the Dyke is at its most impressive and its improved height confirms that it means business. It is not difficult to sit here on a warm summer's day and conjure up pictures from the past: images of gangs of local recruits toiling away with basic tools to build this frontier wall under the supervision of Offa's engineers.

From the triangulation point continue along the Dyke until directed on to the lane to your left-hand side, a measure to preserve a badly crumbling section of Dyke. Maintain your forward direction with the lane passing old rusting farm machinery that has long since ploughed its last furrow.

The path and Dyke go marching on to the north but about ½ mile from the triangulation point take a path on the left passing through a metal gateway. Head about 20 degrees south of west over a field of grass and thistle, a

It is very clear from here that the **Dyke** was designed to look westwards and, however much the line might have been agreed with those who were living on the other side, the control was being exercised from the Mercian side. It should not be thought that the Dyke was garrisoned like the mile castles on Hadrian's Wall; more likely it was patrolled when need arose.

little under the summit of the hill to your left. A track is met that curves round to the right, then left to pass through a gateway. Once through the gate bear left with the track rising and then falling to next hill top. It is a wide track with all the character of an old road.

At the top of the rise the track suddenly disappears in the infuriating manner that they so often do, now you see it, now you don't. In its place are two indistinct paths. Take the south-western line, level walking on a thickly thistled hilltop, so much so that in August when the breeze is wafting away the thistledown it has the appearance of an unseasonal snowstorm.

The hill slopes gently towards a metal gate seen ahead. Once through the gate go forward with a fence on your left to cross a small field to a further gate. Here the track again appears with a fence on the left and remnants of hawthorn hedge on your right. Continue with the gently falling track to pass more discarded machinery; this time a seed driller with husks still remaining in the hopper.

Put out to grass? Farming casualty by Offa's Dyke

Soon the descent steepens and, after bending to the left, falls sharply to pass through a gateway at the bottom

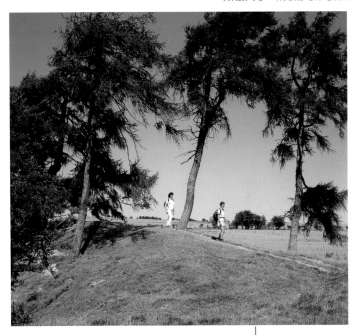

of the slope to join another track. Bear right, passing the old farm at Bwlch. The track runs down into woodland passing the remains of an old quarry. About 30 paces on take the path on your left which descends through the wood at an angle to join a quiet lane.

On Offa's Dyke Path near Llanfair Hill

At the lane turn left and follow it for a little under ¾ mile, shaded by the trees sloping down from Mount Pleasant. On making a junction with a further lane turn left (signed 'Llanfair Waterdine ¼ mile'). There is a great mixture of Welsh and English names both sides of the border, presumably indicating a long period of ebb and flow of people across the Teme seen in the valley bottom to your right. Llanfair Hall is passed away to your left. In a field near here is a large boulder which legend claims was hurled at the church by the Devil in a fit of pique. I can't claim to have inspected this piece of Old Nick's

167

artillery but supposed proof of the story is provided by the impression of his hands in the rock – he must have had quite a grip!

The little church at **Llanfair Waterdine** is worth a few minutes exploration. It features some beautifully embroidered hassocks with a variety of badges, symbols, birds and scenes. Many of the pews have the names of local farms that paid tithes to the church, inscribed in gilt script on the bench ends. The organ is not all that it appears, for hidden within it is an old barrel organ with a small repertoire of hymn tunes; a useful standby when the organist is on holiday! Waterdine is an old border village and its church was rebuilt in the middle of the 19th century. In this connection attention must be drawn to the finely carved altar rails which came from the old church and carries an inscription in Welsh.

Llanfair Waterdine

Llanfair Waterdine is a tiny village, its population just 12 adults and 4 children, the fate of the village school illustrating the decline of some rural communities. In the mid 20th century there were 60 pupils and not long before that a full 100 children were educated there. The school is now the village hall and bears the grand title of Everest Hall, as well it might for Lord Hunt, whose expedition first climbed Everest in 1953, lived but a short distance away.

A local legend (although a similar story crops up elsewhere) concerns a young lad who was given the duty of keeping the birds off the new sown fields. This was a common enough country occupation, but on this occasion somewhat thoughtless since it was fair day, and the fair was a quite irresistible magnet. The temptation to neglect his duties must have been nearly overwhelming, but a strong sense of responsibility made him cast around for someone to take over his irksome task. But everybody was at the fair – everybody that is except the Devil. A deal was done, the Devil would keep the birds off the fields and in exchange would take half the lad's soul as payment to be cashed in at some future date.

The lad ran off to the fair, soon forgetting his bargain with the Devil. The fields were unmolested and no one was any the wiser. Eventually the Devil called in his IOU, before the boy reached manhood, and as a result the young man was buried half in the churchyard and half outside – one half of his soul for God, the other for the Devil.

From the village continue on. Ignore the first turn on the left but on meeting a road coming in from the right bear left (signed 'Monaughty Poeth and Skyborry Green', surely we are in a foreign country?). In about 300 yards take a narrow lane on the left, which rises through woods and then descends to the farm at Graig.

Beyond the farm buildings bear left on a track signed as unsuitable for motor vehicles and continue with this for about 500 yards then turn right with it at a sharp bend, a narrow old winding lane between hedges. There is a long upward stretch between high banks, but what goes up must come down and eventually the crest is reached and the lane falls with the white cottage of Brynorgan seen beneath the hills. The lane meets the road at Selley Cross. Ignore both left and right turns and continue forward, (signed to Clun) soon to meet Offa's Dyke and your starting point.

Tourist information: Offa's Dyke Heritage Centre, West Street, Knighton
Tel: 01547 528753

WALK 19

Croft Castle and the Sun in Splendour

Maps:	1:25,000 Explorer 203 Ludlow; 1:50,000 Landranger 137 Ludlow & Church Stretton
Distance:	3 miles approx
Car parking:	National Trust car park, Croft Castle (grid ref 452656) open to dusk

Basic route: Croft Castle, Croft Ambrey fort, Fishpool Valley

For this walk we make an excursion into neighbouring Herefordshire for a 'lollipop walk' – a visit to a place of interest combined with a shortish walk which can be comfortably covered in a summer afternoon. The walk starts from the National Trust car park in the grounds of Croft Castle.

Croft Castle is found on the B4362 about 2 miles to the east of Mortimer's Cross (A4410) or about 5 miles to the west of the A49 at Woofferton. Mortimer's Cross, although tiny, has an important and lasting place in English history; more of that later.

The castle has an arched gateway in the curtain wall reminiscent of a child's toy fort, an impression that is heightened by the house itself. Here is a splendid mansion, large and square, stone built with great round towers at each corner, its military appearance ameliorated by its Georgian style sash windows and leaded lights. The house is beautifully sited with views to the hills and grounds that are a pleasure to explore. Amongst the attractive features are the Fishpools Valley, an avenue of venerable sweet chestnuts and a walled garden of mellowed brick. Sharing the shelter of these old walls are grape vines, figs, and the everyday vegetables that might be found in any back garden, a pleasing mixture reflecting the continued family occupation of Croft Castle.

Croft Castle – now cared for by the National Trust

To the visitor the house offers panelled rooms, fine plasterwork ceilings, beautifully polished floors and furniture of distinction from past centuries. Family portraits look down upon you from every wall, former residents of this great house, men who had achieved distinction in various fields, their elegant ladies, and of course the children.

The family's connection with Croft dates back to at least the time of the Domesday survey. There was a break from 1746 until 1923 when the property was re-purchased. The church lies so close to the house that on a wet Sunday morning, family worshippers might well leave their front door as the clock started to strike the hour and yet be in their place on time and without need of an umbrella.

The church, with its boxed pews, is full of interest. Its close connection with the great house is quickly apparent. Amongst the memorials the tomb that takes first place is that of Sir Richard Croft and Eleanor his wife. They lived at a time of great conflict when over a long period of years the rival Houses of Lancaster and York pursued their claims to the throne by force of arms.

Sir Richard had battle honours which included Mortimer's Cross 1461, Tewkesbury 10 years later and Stoke (near Newark) in 1487. It was after this last battle (which resulted in the capture of Lambert Simnel,) that Richard was created knight baronet. Richard was Sheriff

The church by Croft Castle

of Herefordshire on several occasions and Governor of the nearby Ludlow Castle, but it is the battle of 1461, fought on his very doorstep that takes our attention.

Sir Richard had lent his support to Edward, the recently orphaned, 19-year old son of Richard, Duke of York. An army of some 5000 men had been assembled and set to guard the road along which the Lancastrian army was obliged to pass and to deny access to the river crossings. It was a strategy that worked with heavy losses to the smaller forces of Lancaster. The legend that has grown up suggests that the Yorkist army's confidence had been greatly increased by the appearance in the wintry February sky of three suns. It was probably a manifestation of the halo effect one occasionally sees, that was taken as a favourable portent, and it led to Edward IV taking the 'sun in splendour' as one of his emblems. Hence Shakespeare's famous pun 'Now is the winter of our discontent made summer by this sun of York' (*Richard III*).

A monument erected in 1799 at Kingsland, just south of Mortimer's Cross refers to the:

'...obstinate, bloody and decisive battle between the ambitious Houses of York and Lancaster on the 2nd Day of February 1461 between the Forces of Edward Mortimer, Earl of March, (afterwards Edward the Fourth) on the side of York and those of Henry the Sixth, on the side of Lancaster.

The King's troops were commanded by Jasper, Earl of Pembroke, Edward commanded his own in person and was victorious. The slaughter was great on both sides, four thousand being left dead on the field and many Welsh persons of the first distinction were taken prisoners among whom was Owen Tudor (Great-Grandfather to Henry VIII, and a descendant of the illustrious Cadwallader) who was afterwards beheaded at Hereford.

Signs of battle – the Monument Inn at Kingsland – the memorial stone below tells the story of the rewards of victory and the penalties of defeat

This was the decisive battle which fixed Edward the Fourth on the Throne of England who was proclaimed King in London on the fifth of March following'.

The Monument Inn uses a painting of the monument as its sign and at Mortimer's Cross the inn signs depict the contestants, armed and armoured together with their respective badges. Altogether an excellent little piece of history retold succinctly in words and pictures.

From the car park go towards the arched gatehouse of the castle enclosure but do not pass through. Turn right and after a short distance cross a cattle grid by way of a kissing gate. Follow a metalled path and soon bear right with this as it rises gently. Once past a large cottage on the left the track becomes rougher and continues on through a metal gateway.

Maintain your direction, roughly northwards, passing some venerable sweet chestnut trees, their trunks twisted and gnarled with age. After a further clump of chestnuts enter the Forestry Commission's Croft Wood where a sign directs you forward to Croft Ambrey on a still rising path. When a crossing track is reached, continue forward soon to emerge from the woods. The steep slopes of Yatton Hill to your left fall to the valley whilst more distant hills roll on towards Wales.

Leave the forest by a five-barred gate and go forward along a bracken edged track with a fence to your right. After a short distance cross a stile on your right (blue waymark) bearing half left and in a few yards scramble up the steep path onto the ramparts of the **hill fort.**

Croft Ambrey hill fort

This hill top fort with its high banked, deeply ditched defences was home to men, women and children of the Iron Age for some 600 years. Archaeologists have discovered evidence of repeated replacement of the wooden gateways which gave access to the fort; as many as 20 renewals confirming the long residential use of the camp. During the years of its occupation the fort was enlarged so that it ultimately covered an area of nearly 40 acres. Within the protection of the compound, which in terms of later years you might regard as a walled town, there were a number of wooden buildings, which like the gates were subject to decay and were repeatedly rebuilt. As we have already seen in the Caer Caradoc walk, this part of the country was coming under pressure as the Romans pushed out their frontiers westwards towards Wales and around AD 50 this beautiful hill top camp, which had been home to upwards of 500 people, became another of history's deserted villages.

On reaching the top of the bank turn right and follow the ramparts eastwards. It is necessary to duck under an ancient oak which has spread its branches wide and low over the bank. Shortly after this merge with a path coming in from the left and turn right on a falling path. A blue waymark confirms you are on the right track. Ignore a right turn. The descent steepens and a small stile is crossed, after which turn right. In 50 yards pass through a gate on the right (blue arrowed) and down a slope to meet a broader track.

Here turn right and after about 100 yards take a forest road to the left which takes a falling, curving passage. There is a good mix of trees; ash, beech, sycamore, larch, Norwegian spruce, and other conifers with honey-suckle spreading itself over bushes. To the right is a deep cleft which surely must carry water but is totally disguised by the thick greenery. The track curves to the right as it is joined by a broad path coming in from the left.

Continue for a further 50 yards before turning right and then, after a few yards left, on a red and blue way-marked path, heading down the Fishpool Valley. Soon the tiny stream widens to produce a series of ponds; an attractive prospect with the trees reflected in the still clear water. Ignore the blue track when it leads off right and keep with the red and green waymarking until after the third pool when the path divides. Take the right branch, red and green marked. The path climbs steadily uphill to emerge close to the car park and your starting point.

It should be mentioned that the National Trust also owns the adjacent Bircher Common and amongst the wildlife mentioned in its handbook are fallow deer, stoats, weasels and polecats which have extended their territory from across the Welsh border.

Tourist information: Castle Street, Ludlow Tel: 01584 875053

Croft Castle (National Trust): House open March weekends from 1pm. Apr–Nov: Weds–Sun. Tea rooms and gardens open from 12. Car park, picnic area, parkland and hill fort open throughout the year

Berrington Hall (National Trust): About 5 miles from Croft. 18th-century house to design of Henry Holland and landscaped by Capability Brown. House open early March weekends from 1pm, otherwise daily, except Thursdays and Fridays, to early November.

WALK 20

Top of the Lot

Maps:	1:25,000 Explorer 217 Long Mynd & Wenlock Edge; 1:50,000 Landranger 138 Kidderminster & Wyre Forest
Distance:	6 miles or 4½ miles
Car parking:	Road side near start of trail (grid ref 607872)

Basic route: Brown Clee Forest Trail (near Cleobury North), Brown Clee Hill, Abdon Burf, Abdon Liberty, High Croft, Monkeys' Fold, Five Springs and return via forest and bridleway

Brown Clee Hill at 1772 feet is the highest point in Shropshire and its seniority should by rights reserve a place for it as the last walk in the book. No disrespect to Brown Clee but that privilege, if that is the word, has been accorded to what at first sight is the strangest landscape in all the county. Brown Clee is high moorland topped by a coronet – steel communication masts beneath which lie the scars of old mines. Its brow is swathed in a bandage of forest with some fine parkland trees on the lower slopes.

To find the start of the walk leave Cleobury North by the Ditton Priors Road, then take a left turn, heading towards the eastern edge of Brown Clee Hill. Just beyond a sharp right bend car parking will be found under trees near the start of the Forest Trail.

From the parking area pass through a five-barred gate by the Forest Trail notice and turn right on a gorse lined path soon curving to the left. There are fine views to the east with the chequer board landscape in late spring broken by the luminescent patterns of oil seed rape midst the darker patches of the pasture.

About 250 yards after entering the forest take the path on the right by a five-barred gate and stile which bears a welcome notice. Head up through woods on a winding track with beech, larch and Norwegian spruce. After climbing for some while pass through a five-barred gate and go forward over a crossing track to take a narrow path through the trees, soon to bear right on a wider track in a less thickly wooded area. The path narrows after crossing a streamlet. Beyond the stream the path bends left and upwards. When a large beech tree is reached make sure you are heading left and uphill.

Confirmation that you are on the right path is given by the humps and bumps of former quarrying activities and with the tops of radio masts seen ahead. A little to the right are the remains of old **mine buildings** ◀.

As you draw level with the mine buildings the masts come fully into view, their great ears cocked in all directions. There is a confusion of paths, sheep runs, on this hillside but if you have hit the right one you should meet the road by a deep pool. Turn left and on reaching a cattle grid continue with the road as it curves round towards the masts.

Before the masts are reached climb the steps on the left to the triangulation point to enjoy the view. The hill is on occasions enveloped in cloud as regular travellers along the A49 will testify. In case this provides wayfinding problems you may like to note the road as an escape route to lower levels.

The ground is rough and heather covered, pockmarked by countless generations of mining and quarrying – coal, stone and iron – fuel to power the sinews of

Amongst the **mine buildings** a row of stones suggest the boundary of a house, and this is confirmed by a clump of rhubarb looking strangely out of place. How long was it since a mine employee took rhubarb and custard for his Sunday lunch on this high and remote hillside?

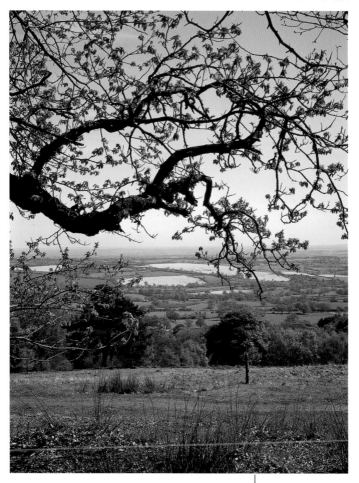

industry. Somehow it is appropriate amongst this guddle of past endeavour that today's communications systems, the modern arteries of commerce, are represented here on this high and windy hill amidst the spoil heaps of the past.

Brown Clee – a view over Shropshire from the forest edge

The horizons are defined by the clarity of the day. Guide books have claimed a view over 14 counties. That is as maybe, but walkers who have explored the high points in these pages will at least be able to spot some familiar landmarks. One such not yet visited is Titterstone Clee Hill, lying to the south with its earth satellite station helping recognition. Closer at hand, about 1½ miles to the south, are the masts of another relay station.

From the triangulation point take the path that runs south-west to reach the fence line in about ¼ mile. Cross an old broken wall boundary and stile which bears the Shropshire Way buzzard.

> **Route A:** For the shorter walk turn left at this fence, following the Shropshire Way (south) for about ¾ mile then bearing left to return to the forest by a metal gate. Pick up the **Main walk** on p178.

Main walk contd: Once over the stile bear right along a raised path which I suspect may have been an old railway (Shropshire Way north-west). Keep with this as it swings to the right and pass through a metal gateway, again Shropshire Way signed.

Follow the broad, easy-to-walk falling track and pass through a further gateway. After 130 yards pass through a metal gate on the left and head west of south over a field. The path rises but in a few yards flattens out and heads towards a gate in the field boundary. Maintain forward direction to reach a fence and pass over it (a track and quarry cottage are seen below to the right). Continue forward with bracken on a falling hillside to your right. As the fence at the end of the field is reached the path curves to the right to meet a gateway and the road.

Turn left along the bendy lane and follow it for about ¼ mile, passing Brown Clee House. A barrel, set at a point where the road bends, bears the legend 'Cobblers Dingle'. A few yards beyond this a footpath is indicated off left over a stile. The path bears roughly south-east, climbing steeply. Pass through a line of trees and maintain a diagonal right direction over a field. As height is regained the moorland character of the western side of Brown Clee Hill is seen with its deeply carved clefts through which little streams run. At the top right corner of the field a stile gives on to a lane. Here turn left on a rough metalled way between high banks. Towards the top of the rise, with Woodbank Cottage on the left and High Croft on the right, continue forward over a fence to follow what is now a green lane.

At the end of this lane cross by a metal gate and turn half right to follow a wide path with a fence on your right and beyond, the masts on Clee Burf. The track winds round the flank of the hill. To your left is the strangely named Monkeys' Fold. Continue with the path and when the fence line falls back a metal gate is reached bearing the Shropshire Way sign. Pass through the gate and continue forward to a line of trees and a further gate. A little to the west the map announces **Five Springs** ▶.

Pass through the metal gateway (this is where **Route A** rejoins the **Main walk**) and go forward on a

Five Springs, like fingers on a hand, issue from the bracken covered hillside – cool clear water, rather shallow in a dry summer but nevertheless still running. It is said to be good to drink but stories of sheep's liver fluke come to mind and the temptation might be resisted.

*In memoriam –
Boyne Water under
Brown Clee Hill*

181

broad falling track close to the edge of the wood ignoring turns to left and right. After about ¼ mile a gate by the house at Black Bank will be seen. Do not pass through the gate but turn right, downhill, on an indistinct grassy track. When this briefly levels out by three large beeches in a huddle, bear left continuing down the hillside on a track which becomes more distinct and with a stream hidden away in a deep cleft to your right.

Arriving at a pretty little pool on your left go through the gate and forward with a hard surfaced and gently rising track. Soon another pool is found to the right landscaped in memory of the 10th Viscount Boyne, KCVO, KStJ, JP 1931–95.

Continue with the tree and shrub edged estate road and in 300 yards, as it is joined by another, bear northwards, now lined with parkland trees including gnarled and knobbly trunked sweet chestnuts, introduced to Britain by the Romans. Keep ahead to reach the lane in about ¾ mile and then forward to your starting point.

Tourist information: Castle Street, Ludlow Tel: 01584 875053

WALK 21

The Land Man Made

Maps:	1:25,000 Explorer 203 Ludlow; 1:50,000 Landranger 138 Kidderminster & Wyre Forest
Distance:	3½ miles approx
Car parking:	Close to summit (grid ref 593775). See text for access
Toilets:	Nearest at Cleehill village near view point close to Victoria Inn on A4117

Basic route: Clee Hill quarries summit, Giant's Chair, Callowgate, semi-circuit of lower flanks to Incline to return to quarry

The Clee Hills are rich in mineral wealth and here man, having dug deep into the earth's treasure chest, has in the past scattered the packing and forgotten to replace the lid. The evidence of centuries of the search for coal, iron and stone is seen in a landscape pitted and dotted with an uneven surface of lumps and bumps, the remains of old quarry buildings – large and small. Stone is still extracted from the Clee Hills for road making and a coal seam has recently been uncovered.

This is a walk that starts from the top of the hill (well nearly) so that the splendid view offered from the summit is obtained with little effort for those with their own transport. From Cleehill village take the Ludlow Road (A4117) and turn right to Dhustone. Follow the long narrow road uphill, beyond the village and pursue this to the old quarries, turning to the right with the road to park by the quarry.

All around is a landscape that has been raided by man and left in untidy heaps for nature to do its best to heal the wounds. It must be said that the area has a perverse interest of its own. More recent work with the cleaner cut of modern machinery has had different results.

You are parked in a dramatic lunar landscape, an impression greatly heightened by the radar masts and the white dome of an earth satellite station perched high above a former quarry. Here countless millions of tons of stone and spoil have been removed. The great scoop of the former quarry is almost neat enough to encourage the thought that we are seeing a partly constructed sports stadium of Olympic proportions. From the eastern end of the quarry, near a pool head up an incline to reach the top edge of the quarry. Bear left along its rim heading towards the earth satellite station. Head half left, passing the installations to your right, to make for the triangulation point.

From the summit (1749 feet) the views are wide with a circle of hills fading into the distance. Beyond Ludlow rise the tree covered hills that make up part of the Mortimer Forest. To the north beyond the mosaic of the farmland rises Brown Clee Hill with its own tall masts. The equipment of the Civil Aviation Authority's tracking station gives off an incessant mosquito like hum and notices warn of high voltage.

Cheek by jowl with today's technology are the remains of an Iron Age hill fort, but somehow it escapes proper notice amongst all the upheaval of the mining operations and the scattered stone that litters the slopes. The area must have been fairly well populated in its day for the fort is amongst the largest with other, albeit smaller, forts on Abdon Burf, Clee Burf and Nordy Bank.

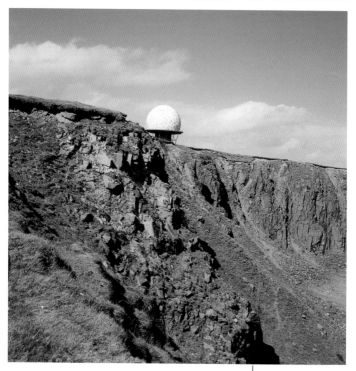

Titterstone Clee Hill – earth satellite station above the great amphitheatre of the quarry

From the triangulation point bear right along the little path to the Giant's Chair, a rocky and uncomfortable seat that looks north to Brown Clee Hill. From here there is a steeply scrambling descent that is best avoided. At first sight there seems no clear path for the next leg of the walk. Turn eastwards until you can comfortably swing to the north and make for the red-roofed cottage seen below at Callowgate.

Looking back shows the ostrich egg-like shape of the satellite station sitting in a giant's egg cup. After descending through the bracken, pass through tufted grass and about 200 yards or so short of the cottage bear left on a broad track (not all that obvious at first – but wheel marks will give the clue). The path heads roughly south-west soon to pass through bracken. The way terraces under the lower flanks of the hill, making a long slow curving semi-circuit.

The summit rises darkly above a sea of green, its upper slopes banded by a wide black vein of rock. The satellite stations appear over one shoulder. Continue with your track, ignoring all turns to left and right. After a period of fairly level walking height is gradually regained and the path levels out again. Beneath the western edge of the hill ahead, on the skyline, will be seen the steeply shelved slopes of Clee Hill, still being quarried and neatly cut like slices of cake, a sharpness not normally found in nature.

After a while the little settlement of Titterstone comes into view. As you draw level with this the path leads to the old incline that carried the light railway. Go forward to this, turn left to follow the incline back to the hill top. At the top of the incline a crumbling mass of old buildings remain, grist to the mill for future industrial archaeologists. Maybe today's graffiti will cause them more problems than the industrial remains. Bear right on the mine track with the buildings to your left.

The track curves left up the hill and after passing under a broken arch of a bridge bear left with the road to make a return to your starting point.

Tourist information: Castle Street, Ludlow Tel: 01584 875053

NOTES

LISTING OF CICERONE GUIDES